Praise for

The 7 Great Prayers
for a Lifetime of Hope and Blessings

The following letters are from readers like you whose lives have been changed by *The 7 Great Prayers for a Lifetime of Hope and Blessings*. These letters are from people who received our original self-published edition, which came with a prayer CD.

Finally, Hope

I want to let you know that I've been praying your prayers all the time, morning and evening. Last night my dreams were full of strength and self-esteem, unlike my dreams before which were of lack, fear, and insecurity. I truly believe God sent me to you.
—*Karen*

Closer to God

I want to thank you for *The 7 Great Prayers*. I read the book and then listened to your CDs for 21 days as you suggested. It really does work! I found that during the course of daily life, the seven prayers would just come to me and this certainly helped me get closer to God.

When I would walk into my home after work I would immediately start playing the CD. I couldn't wait to hear your prayers, they are comforting and inspiring.

God bless you, your wife, and your family. —*Lucille*

No More Fear

My niece from the Netherlands bought two copies of your book and CDs. She sent one set to me and she has the other set. She came to know about *The 7 Great Prayers* through me. She has her own business and after listening to your CD she says she has lost her fear of the future.

With regards to me, I just received a major financial blessing. When I arrived home, I went to my room and cried hard, thanking God over and over again for giving me this big financial blessing. It is true, "ask and you will receive."

Thank you Paul. God bless you and your family! —*Maria*

Removing the Stress

I loved reading your book. I use your prayer CD going to and from work. My work is eighteen miles each way, so I have great listening time. One of the wonderful things that *The 7 Great Prayers* book and CD have done is to enable me to pray more spontaneously. I don't have to pause and think what my next prayer will be.

The *7 Great Prayers* book and CD have completely taken away the stress and pressure I used to feel before I prayed. Amen.

Thank you Paul and Tracey McManus. May God bless you every day in every way. —*Ernest*

Just in Time

Before Thanksgiving I was in such financial distress that I literally fell to the ground and prayed for financial relief. I then remembered *The 7 Great Prayers* and I prayed them for 21 consecutive days. Even before the 21 days were up I started thinking and acting differently; I was changed. I get so excited every time I pray along with your prayer CD. Now, I literally *expect* God's blessings and miracles in my life. This has been so transforming. Thank you and God bless you! —*Shirley*

For the Whole Family

I received your book and prayer CD and really love them. My children are even saying the prayers; they hold their attention! (They are five and two and this is no easy task!) They love to say *The 7 Great Prayers* when they are going to bed and it really helps them focus their attention on God before falling asleep. They fall asleep happier and easier when they do this. Thank you for everything! —*Alanna*

Noticing a Big Difference in My Life

I have been using your prayer book and CD at home and at work and am noticing a big difference in my life. I was surfing on the Internet and believe I was brought to you by "divine guidance."

What I love about your prayers, book, and CD are that they have every area of my life covered and things that have bothered me in the past are now affirmed in a positive light, benefiting me and glorifying God. Thank you, Paul and Tracey, for creating the prayers and CD and allowing God to use you as a vessel, helping a great many along the way! —*Ronda*

Love Listening to the CD

I played my CD right when I got it, I was so excited. As I was washing the dishes and listening to my CD, words can't really explain how I started to feel within. I suppose God's love must have built up inside me because halfway through the CD I started saying "thank you God for loving me and looking after me," and the next second I was crying tears of joy and happiness deep within me. Wow! What a feeling and what a moment. It was pure bliss!

I listened to the second part of the CD when I went to bed; the music is great and the affirmative prayers I remembered from your book kept going through my mind until I fell asleep. God bless all the souls and the planet. —*Heather*

Things Are Turning Around

Ever since finding and taking up your method of prayer, things have begun turning around for my family. Not that things were bad, but there were situations that needed God's hand in them and He has answered.

My daughter has obtained a new job that pays more. Both of my sons are doing better at school, and a relationship with my ex-in-laws healed. Now that's a true miracle. Things are not perfect, but they will keep improving with continued prayer. Of that I am certain. —*Ellen*

The 7 Great Prayers

Vanguard Press
A Member of the Perseus Books Group

The Simple, Powerful Way to Change Your Life

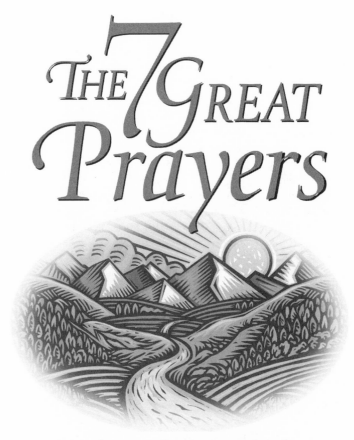

The 7 Great Prayers

For a Lifetime of Hope and Blessings

Paul and Tracey McManus

Published by Vanguard Press
A Member of the Perseus Books Group

DESIGN BY JANE RAESE
Set in 12-point Dante

Cataloging-in-Publication Data for this book is available
from the Library of Congress.
ISBN 978-1-59315-549-0

Vanguard Press books are available at special discounts for bulk purchases
in the U.S. by corporations, institutions, and other organizations.
For more information, please contact the Special Markets Department
at the Perseus Books Group, 2300 Chestnut Street, Suite 200,
Philadelphia, PA 19103, or call (800) 810-4145, ext. 5000,
or e-mail special.markets@perseusbooks.com.

1 3 5 7 9 10 8 6 4 2

Contents

Part Three:
The 7 Great Prayers *57*

Dear Friend

On a beautiful fall day, October 8, 2008, we celebrated our twenty-fifth wedding anniversary in a quaint restaurant on the Connecticut shoreline.

Our gift to each other that anniversary day was a simple one. It was a galley printout of the newly updated manuscript of the book you now hold in your hands, *The 7 Great Prayers for a Lifetime of Hope and Blessings.*

Up until our anniversary, we had made copies of our book at a Kinko's Copy Center, one after another, until we had sold and shipped tens of thousands of copies of the book to people in 163 countries, making it one of the top self-published books ever.

God gave us a precious gift, and it's our life's purpose to share this book and the 7 Great Prayers with as many of God's children as possible. We knew we couldn't keep making copies by ourselves. We needed more help. We needed a publisher to bring our book to bookstores and churches worldwide.

As we celebrated our twenty-fifth anniversary and the new bookstore edition of our book, we thanked God for the people who were brought into our lives to help us offer the message of the 7 Great Prayers to the millions of people who need them.

We are certain God would want nothing more than for you to read this book again and again, and then use the 7 Great Prayers every day for the rest of your life.

What would give God even more pleasure is if after you read this book, you share it with a friend or a loved one. (The Seventh Great Prayer is "God, Help Me Help You.") By sharing your copy, you'll be introducing that person to life-changing affirmative prayers and powerful ways in which to live the abundant and blessed life God wants for all His children.

TRACEY AND I DEDICATE THIS BOOK and the 7 Great Prayers to you. From the bottom of our hearts, we know that you can live a hopeful and blessed life, and God can help you do so. This is the life God wants for you!

Tracey and I are just like you. We're all God's children. We've been through many of the same financial hardships, family challenges, relationship issues, and health concerns you may have already experienced or may be currently going through. We want to let you know that, whatever challenge you may face in life, God is always with you to comfort, heal, and inspire, and to give you the strength you need, when you need it.

It's our sincerest hope that through the power of affirmative prayer and the 7 Great Prayers, you become closer to God and live a more joyful life, and that you and yours are always blessed with God's gifts and love.

May God bless you and yours always. With love,

Acknowledgments

We owe our greatest thanks to God. We had no idea when we began that the 7 Great Prayers would touch and change so many lives around the world. We thank God and ask for His continued support, strength, and love as we continue our mission to help others.

We give special thanks to our beloved children: Casey, Kevin, and Katherine McManus. We also appreciate the support of David Ward, Anny Ward, and Katie Lagana; my parents, Jack and Jane McManus; and Tracey's parents, Lynne and Andy Green.

The 7 Great Prayers and this book are a collaborative effort in which God worked through many people. Tracey and I thank all those listed here who supported our efforts.

David Addison, Early Advantage, Anne Alderman Person, Pat Babbage, Joyce Barney, Steve and Michelle Baeir, Mark and Carol Boland, Danny Bouchotte, Chris Brown, Sylvia Brown, Susan Cinquegrana, Scott Conover, Roger Cooper, Chris Corcoran, Jim Daly, Frank DeLucia, Olivia DeVito, Jack Dudley, Charlene Ellison, Lois Fahey, Amanda Ferber, Andre and Mark Fitzgerald, Fred Gatti, John Glaiser, Matty Goldberg, Carl Green, Richard Hastings, Terry Hastings, Mary Hunt, Diane and Mike Iorfino, Lynn Jacobs, Barb Jagoe, Shane Keegan, MaryAnn and Joe Kelley, Kathy Kingsley, Arthur Klebanoff, Chris Koch, Nick Kopik, Georgina Levitt, Doug Lewis, Mark and Wendy Lionetti, Jim and Pat Lusher, Lynchburg College, Maggie and Ken Mahoney, Cindy and Mark Manning, Christine Marra, Marcy Michaud, Doug McDonald, Ken McGovern, Debbie and Tom McInerney, Chris McManus, Mark McManus, Cindy Miller, Bill Mirbach, Newtown Scholarship Association, Joan Ochs, Dan O'Connel, Terry Pfeiffer, Mike Rittlinger, Karen Rowel, Jack Ryan, Steve Saffel, Brad Sainsbury, Jennifer Schilling, Lou and Kate Sclafani, University of Scranton, Teresa Shappell, Al Smith, Ivan Sokolovich, Jeff Tolson, Sandy Trado, Kim and Beth Uniacke, Peter Vogt, Wendy VonDerLinn, Todd Walters, Mary Walker, Jeff Weiss, Payson Welch, Shane Workman, and the many others who helped make this book a reality. Thank you all, and God bless you and yours!

PART ONE

Our Story

As we all know, the blessings of life can come and go. So the big question is, how do you handle life's uncertainties? Our answer has been, with gratitude and prayer. During good times and hard times, the 7 Great Prayers and affirmative prayers have helped our family live a hopeful and blessed life.

Before creating the 7 Great Prayers, we were living what we would call a normal life. Tracey and I were high school sweethearts. As the years passed, we were blessed with three wonderful children and were living in a quaint New England town in Connecticut.

My career started in New York City in advertising. Then I worked for software and technology companies, where I specialized in marketing. Tracey was a professional photographer who took family portraits in outdoor settings.

The Beginning of the
7 Great Prayers

The first of the 7 Great Prayers came to Tracey and me while we lay awake in the middle of the night after I'd lost my job due to the dot-com bust of 2000. We'd lost all our savings, the bill collectors were banging on our door, and we were losing the home of our dreams. We were paralyzed with fear, so Tracey suggested that we thank God for what we had: our health, each other, and three beautiful children.

This prayer giving thanks helped a lot. It was better to focus on the good and what we had than to focus on what we had lost and were losing. The prayer helped so much that Tracey and I sat down and—based on a lifetime of spiritual reading and from our shared experiences—created six more simple and powerful prayers that helped reduce the stress, anxiety, and depression that we were going through. These prayers gave us hope. They kept us positive.

They kept us happy and strengthened our love.

The Secret

Tracey and I discovered the secret of the ages, which is that you become what you think about most. Great thinkers such as Robert Collier, James Allen, and Earl Nightingale wrote much on this subject. Tracey and I applied this miraculous formula with prayer to our own lives and things soon got much better in all areas of our lives.

Since everyone goes through difficult times at some point, we shared these 7 Great Prayers with friends and family who had lost a job, had lost a loved one, were going through a divorce, were experiencing health problems, were lonely and looking for love, and such. Sure enough, these prayers helped them.

Sharing the Secret

I built a simple one-page Web site so we could share these 7 Great Prayers with anyone who needed help. People loved them. The prayers provided inspiration, strength, comfort, and joy. These people started sharing the 7 Great Prayers with their friends and family, and the next thing you know, 20 million people had visited this Web site.

Tracey and I received thousands of e-mails. People shared their stories about how the 7 Great Prayers changed their lives. They wanted more, so we sat down and wrote a book.

Although I wrote much of this book, my writing is heavily influenced by Tracey. Whereas I'm the type of person who has to think, read, and talk about how best to live a spiritual life, Tracey just does it naturally. God bless her! I wish I had this gift. Tracey has a simple and positive outlook on life, family, and God that I incorporate into all my writing. *The 7 Great Prayers for a Lifetime of Hope and Blessings* is a collaborative effort. In the chapters about the 7 Great Prayers, you'll find inspiring stories written by Tracey.

After we wrote the book, Tracey and I recorded onto a CD the 7 Great Prayers and a hundred or so positive affirmations, with beautiful background music. These prayers are for all faiths. We found that when people are under crisis, praying can be very difficult. Sometimes it is easier to press the play button and just listen to the prayers, so we made the CD for people to play in their car, while walking or exercising, and before going to bed.

Word Spread

We went to a Kinko's Copy Center and made copies of the book. In no time we'd printed 60,000 books and shipped them to countries around the world, including Canada, Australia, Japan, the Philippines, India, and

Nigeria. *The 7 Great Prayers* became Kinko's #1 self-published book.

We believe that God is behind the 7 Great Prayers, and we've put our complete faith and trust in Him. We're not preachers; we're just regular people. And for some reason, we were inspired to write and share these 7 Great Prayers. We've seen amazing things in our own lives and in the lives of those who have used them.

As we prepare this newly revised version, it's early 2009 and the entire world is in an economic crisis, one that may last for years. With the world in a financial meltdown, these prayers are needed more than ever.

Through the grace of God we were led to a longtime friend and business associate, David Ward. Then David led us to Arthur Klebanoff, who led us to Vanguard Press, Roger Cooper, Georgina Levitt, and Amanda Ferber. Tracey and I have given thanks that we are with this great group of people. Together we are unified in our mission to bring the 7 Great Prayers to as many people around the world as possible because we know these prayers will bring hope, peace, and blessings to all who use them.

You are in *our* prayers.

A Powerful Way to Change Your Life

Give the 7 Great Prayers a try. Use them for 21 days. Maybe you have a friend or family member who is going through a difficult time. If that's the case, share the prayers with him or her.

These prayers help if you need hope or change in your life in regards to better financial security, improving relationships with family and friends, and addressing health matters, depression, stress, anxiety and more. Use them daily. Once you repeat them for 21 consecutive days, the prayers will become as natural as breathing and you'll discover that you are happier and living a hopeful and blessed life.

Before we learn about the 7 Great Prayers, however, let's learn how to tap into the power of God.

PART TWO

*Tap into the Power
of God*

1

Why We Wrote This Book

Tracey and I wrote this book to help you get closer to God and tap into God's power through the use of the 7 Great Prayers and the accompanying affirmative prayers.

An affirmative prayer is a request to God expressed in a personal and positive way and in the present tense. It is said as though God has *already* granted your request. Praying affirmatively is a powerful way to pray.

Here are a couple of examples of affirmative prayers:

Thank you God for blessing me with health, wealth, and happiness.

God, you are with me right now. You give me
    comfort and strength.

When you use the 7 Great Prayers and the affirmative
prayers along with the provided prayer techniques, it will
be easy for you to tap into the power of God. God is *always* with you—always. The secret to living a hopeful
and blessed life is to connect with God and tap into
God's almighty power. This book will show you how.

When you connect with God, you will gain comfort
and strength and achieve success in all areas of your life.
When praying and being with God, it's imperative that
you always think and pray *positively.*

Many researchers who study the lives of men and
women who have achieved success or overcome serious
life challenges—such as the loss of a job, financial hardship, or a life-threatening health issue—will tell you that
these amazing people have transcended their difficulties
through the power of positive thinking and affirmative
prayer.

Think Positively and Be Blessed

In the book *Think and Grow Rich,* Napoleon Hill studied
the lives of Henry Ford, Andrew Carnegie, and Thomas
Edison. Each of these successful people shared a com-

mon trait: No matter how great the challenge or horrifying the obstacle they faced, each connected to their Higher Power (God). They thought and acted positively. You can think and act positively too!

We all know people who seem to think and act positively naturally, as though they were born with this ability. But they weren't born this way. Most likely they lived in households and environments where the people around them thought positively; living under those conditions, they naturally learned to do the same. When faced with a challenge or problem, they think and pray positively, and their prayers are answered.

The rest of us—myself included—need to work hard to think and act positively. This book, and the 7 Great Prayers included within it, will help you think and act positively, which will attract more of God's blessings into your life.

Your mind is like a magnet—it attracts into your life whatever you think about most. Think, act, and feel negatively, and you'll attract negative people and events into your life.

One of the gifts that God gave all of us is *choice*: the choice to do good or to do evil; the choice to think and act positively or to live negatively.

One of the chief objectives of this book is to make thinking and praying positively into a *lifetime* habit. A positive mental attitude can be developed and maintained by following the prayer processes revealed in this book. You can literally *attract* blessings into your life each and every day through prayer, affirmations, and positive thinking.

Turn Off the Bad News and Turn On the Good

Regrettably, we are exposed to negative thinking every day, and it seems as if it's escalating all the time. For many people, negative thinking begins the second the alarm goes off and the clock radio starts spouting the morning news updates: a tragic nighttime fire, a morning traffic accident, bad financial news—within minutes your mind is filled with negative thinking.

Next you are subjected to the complaints of family members, friends, and coworkers. All the negative thoughts expressed in your presence have a profound effect on you. They hurt your self-esteem, promote negative thinking, and hinder your future and your ability to overcome life's challenges.

The only way to overcome life's inevitable challenges is to think and act positively. Tracey and I have found that the easiest and most effective way to switch from negative to positive thinking is to use the 7 Great Prayers and the affirmative prayers that accompany them.

In Robert Collier's book *The Secret of the Ages,* he tells us that the secret of the ages is that *you become what you think about most.* So turn off the TV. Turn off the radio. Put aside the newspaper. Limit the negative thinking you expose yourself to. Instead, start thinking and praying positively.

The Secret: The 7 Great Prayers

Using the 7 Great Prayers and the affirmation prayers in this book, you can create your own personal prayer program. Need greater financial stability or security? Love? Health? Friends? Purpose? Healing? Connect with God through the 7 Great Prayers to find your path to all these things and more.

The truly successful person who attracts blessings into his or her life thinks and acts positively. Positive attracts positive. Negative attracts negative. The second you start thinking negatively, you need to make a conscious choice to hop off the negative train and hop onto the positive train.

And the fastest way to change your life—to change what you are becoming—is to tap into the power of God. God is good. God is great. There is no negative when it comes to God.

It's all good.

Who Is God?

This book and the 7 Great Prayers are not a religious philosophy. Much of what makes the 7 Great Prayers so great is that these powerful prayers inspire *all* people and *all* faiths, so simply adapt them to your faith and beliefs.

The first edition of this book was shipped to every race and creed on earth. We received orders from Catholics in Boston, Hindus in India, Christians in Korea, Australia, and Africa, Muslims in Pakistan, Jews in Israel, and agnostics in Iceland—all these people, from 163 countries, used *The 7 Great Prayers* to connect with the God of their understanding. With this new connection with God, they are on the path to living a hopeful and blessed life.

All faiths—and most people on this planet—believe in God, a Higher Power, a supreme intelligence, something greater and more powerful than us. If you believe in God—if you believe in the power of prayer—the 7 Great Prayers and this book are for you.

The Power of Prayers and Affirmations

So, how do you tap into the power of God? You do it through prayer. If you want more power in any area of your life, pray more often. Pray every day and throughout the day. And when you pray include short, positive affirmation prayers.

The simple definition of prayer is *a sincere request to God in words or thought*. The key word in this definition is *sincere*. Mindlessly reciting a lengthy prayer from memory is not effective when compared to a simple, focused prayer expressed earnestly and with love.

The simple definition of an affirmation is *a statement asserting that something is true and exists*.

Affirmations tend to use the word *I* and are focused on the individual who is saying the affirmation. Affirmations can call out to God or request God's help in making the thing you are asserting become true.

For example, here's a powerful affirmation that we'd say to start the morning when our kids were young. We would hold hands and shout:

I feel happy, healthy, and terrific!

We suggest that you and your loved ones start your day with this affirmation and repeat it as many times as you want.

When saying your prayers and affirmations, it's important that you use emotion and enthusiasm. Be enthusiastic—tap into God within.

Even if you don't feel happy, healthy, and terrific, fake it. Fake it until you make it. Try it. Right now if possible. It's virtually impossible not to start feeling happier, healthier, and more terrific after saying the preceding affirmation out loud with a smile on your face.

How to Accomplish Your Goals

To accomplish any goal—greater happiness, better health, more wealth, or a closer relationship with God—you need to develop the proper mindset. We want to help you get that proper mindset and keep it with you all day long.

It is a well-established fact that repetition of thought in the form of daily prayers and affirmations will dramatically increase your ability to achieve your goals and attract into your life the blessings you desire.

Do you like yourself? Do you have good self-esteem? Are you confident? If not, it's going to be difficult for you to achieve your goals. Liking yourself, believing in yourself, and feeling good about your life will be critical to your success in all areas of your life. You will need confidence. You will need to believe in yourself and your ability to overcome and succeed. The good news is, you can do it, and it's all easier when you ask and accept God's help.

Taking action is critical—prayers without actions are not prayers but just wishes. The 7 Great Prayers, combined with the affirmations in this book, will give you the confidence and belief in yourself that you will need to take the actions necessary to make your dreams come true so that you can live the blessed life that you, as a child of God, were born to live.

2

How to Attract Blessings into Your Life

The dictionaries define *blessing* as a thing or an event conducive to your happiness and your welfare. It's natural for all of us to desire happiness and to want our needs (our welfare) taken care of. When we are happy and our needs are being met, we are living an abundant and blessed life—the life we were born to live.

God Wants You to Be Blessed

And God blessed them, saying, "Be fruitful, and multiply, and
fill the waters in the seas, and let fowl multiply in the earth."
— GEN. 1:22

When God created humans,
he made them in the likeness of God.
— GEN. 5:1

When Tracey and I think of God, we sometimes like to add an extra *o* to *God*, making the word into *Good*. Our God is a good God.

Your God is a good God. To live an abundant and blessed life, there is no room for a vengeful and judging God.

God is your father and friend. Would you consider a father who is vengeful and judging to be a great father? Is this the type of friend you would want to have? Of course not! You would want your parents and friends to be loving, accepting, and nonjudgmental. So if your image of God is not one of acceptance, love, strength, and support, please change that picture right now.

If you want to change your life and live a more plentiful life, one full of God's blessings, we ask that you think of God only in a positive way. God is on your side, and God is good. God is great. With God on your side, all is well.

The 7 Great Prayers are designed to connect you to God in a good and positive way. Think of God as good. Think and know that God is always with you—shielding you from all negativity and attracting *only* good into your life.

Know What You Want

The starting point for attracting blessings into your life is to know what blessings you want.

Remember, God has given us the gift of choice. God has not planned your life, for good or bad; instead, God has given you the power of choice. So use it. Take moments throughout the day, week, month, and year to step back and decide what it is that you really want.

Once you know what you want, the next step is to ask yourself *why* you want it. The clearer the picture you can form of what you want and why you want it, the better. Again, your mind is like a powerful magnet—it attracts into your life what you think and pray about most.

The easiest way to make this mental image clearer is to list the reasons why you want a particular blessing or why you want to achieve a particular goal. Write a list, just as you would in making a shopping list or your daily to-do list. The act of writing is important and will be discussed in further detail later. For now, though, just write what blessing you want and why you want it.

I suggest that you purchase a spiral notebook and dedicate that notebook to the 7 Great Prayers. Also, Part Four has a prayer journal for just this purpose. After reading the next section, please pause your reading and turn to the back of this book and start your list.

Please take ownership of this book. Do not treat it like a library book, where you take extra care to make sure you don't damage it. You'll get a lot more from *The 7 Great Prayers for Lifetime of Hope and Blessings* if you actively participate in your reading. One of the best ways to engage your entire being with your reading is to underline important words and sentences when you come upon them. In the margins of the book, write any ideas you may have while reading a particular passage. The more you underline, mark with an asterisk, and write notes in the margin, the better you'll retain and use what you learn.

So go get a pen now and start marking up this book from here on. With pen in hand, please turn to Part Four and start your list of blessing *wants* as well as *why* you want them. Do not read any further until you turn to the back of this book and create your blessing list.

Wealth Blessings

In the first edition of this book, in which the prayers were requested by more than a million people, a large percentage of those people were in some sort of financial hardship, whether due to losing their job, their savings, or even their home. We were flooded with e-mails asking how to pray for financial blessings. We also received requests for suggestions on how to pray for happiness, healing, and a closer relationship with God. But for the moment, we'd like to talk about wealth.

In the fall of 2008, the entire world went through a financial meltdown. Countries, businesses, and families went through financial crises. So if you seek the blessings of wealth or financial stability, realize that you are not alone.

Focus on the Blessings You Have

Our first recommendation is to focus on the wealth—the abundance—that you already have. Two words used in the definition of wealth are *abundant supply*. So being wealthy isn't all about money; it's about having an abundant supply.

You can be wealthy with an abundant supply of health, family, happiness, friends, work, social fulfillment, and more. Areas in your life are already abundant, so focus on those areas. Say prayers of thanks and gratitude.

Use the 7 Great Prayers and the simple techniques in this book, and you will find your path through your financial challenges. All our paths are unique. The 7 Great Prayers will help you find *your* path. When and how you'll find your path is God's job—your job is to pray, think and talk positively, and take action.

Yes, just as important as praying the 7 Great Prayers is that you take *action*—no matter what blessing you want in your life. Financial, health, relationship, and any other blessings you desire require action on your part.

It's All How You Look at It

In regard to bringing additional wealth into your life, you must have a proper perspective about what wealth is. For many, wealth is a luxurious home with a palatial entrance, a swimming pool in the back, and nice cars in the driveway. These are just material possessions. For Tracey and me, wealth is a state of being—a state of mind.

Again, the definition of wealth is *abundant supply.* This is why we use the word *abundant* in various places in this book—we also use the word *abundant* in many of our affirmation prayers found in the back of this book.

One of the primary goals of this book is to help you live a more abundant and blessed life. It's our desire that you have abundance in all areas of your life. But *balance* is key. Excess in any area with a lack in another—for example, lots of money but no family, happiness, or friends—is not good.

Before we started using the 7 Great Prayers, there was a time when Tracey and I had absolutely no abundance when it came to material possessions. We'd lost our home. We ran tag sales and sold much of our furniture and many of our possessions. Our bank accounts were empty. We were flat broke.

We were *below* flat broke.

When you lose everything, you get depressed if you don't step back and start appreciating what you *do* have. So we changed the way we looked at things. We thanked God because we had our health, each other, friends, family, and more. Next thing you know, because we changed the way we looked at life, because we lived in a state of gratitude, our lives changed.

Tracey and I both found new jobs, we were led to a new place to live, and we were better able to pay our bills. Everything changed for us financially when we changed our focus from lack of finances to the abundance of love and family.

This same thinking, this same change in the way you look at life, this state of showing gratitude works if you need more love, health, or purpose in your life as well. Give gratitude for what you have, and what you want to be blessed with will follow.

Please join us in our goal to have all God's children living a hopeful and blessed life.

3

My 7 Great Prayers
Commitment

Now that you've determined that you want a life of
greater abundance, it's time to make the leap. By signing
your name to the following, you make this commitment—to yourself.

> To get closer to God, to tap into God's power,
> and to live an abundant and blessed life, I
> commit to God that I will pray the 7 Great
> Prayers every day.

I know that God rewards those who never
quit. So I will pray without ceasing.

_____

Your name

Where two or three are gathered together in my name,
there am I in the midst of them.
—MATT. 18:20

Join people from around the world and take the 21-
Day Prayer Challenge, found in Part Four. If possible, we
recommend that you take the challenge with a partner
or group and commit to one another. It isn't necessary to
have a prayer partner when you take the 21-Day Prayer
Challenge, but it can be even more rewarding when
shared. To get you started, Tracey and I have signed our
names; as authors of this book, we commit to being your
prayer partners.

_____

_____

_____

Your prayer partner's name

Please note that the 21-Day Prayer Challenge works best when you take the challenge while reading this book, not after you read it. Again, you can find the 21-Day Prayer Challenge in Part Four.

4

The 7 Steps for a Lifetime
of Hope and Blessings

What blessings do you want? Do you want to be healthier? Do you want the blessing of love? Purpose in life? Companionship? A job? Do you want the blessing of healing, be it physical, mental, or financial?

There are seven steps to attaining a closer relationship with God, a relationship in which you can simply and easily tap into God's power to live a hopeful and blessed life. These steps are outlined in this chapter.

Step One

Set a goal. Have a clear picture of what blessings you want.

Remember, you become what you think and pray about most. Your mind works best when it has goals. For example, we should all want to be happy, healthy, and in love, to enjoy work and life, and to be wealthy in the broadest sense.

You should strive for balance in your goals. If you spend all your time working and neglect your health, family, or loved ones, your life is not balanced. The wonderful part of putting balance into your life is that the more balanced you become overall, the easier it is to achieve the particular blessing you currently lack.

Step Two

Tap into your unique God-given gifts.

Take a moment and reflect on what are commonly referred to as your *God-given* gifts. Each person's God-given gifts are different from those of another. What are yours? Write them down—right now—on a separate piece of paper, in the back of this book, in your 7 Great Prayers spiral notebook, or in the space provided here.

Thinking about and discovering your God-given gifts will help you find your life's purpose. The more you use your unique God-given gifts, the more you'll enjoy your life. You'll also find it easier to attract into your life the blessings you desire. God-given gifts can include an inherent love for the outdoors, the ability to get along with people, or a skill of any sort, such as cooking, carpentry, writing, or caring for others.

MY GOD-GIVEN GIFTS

_____

_____

_____

_____

_____

_____

Step Three

Live in a state of gratitude. Always look for the good in life.

Perhaps you've lost your job, but you have a loving family and good health. Give God thanks for what you do have, and give God thanks in advance for the gainful employment that will soon come.

Do not focus on what you lack; instead, focus on all that you have. In time, God will supply what is lacking. The more you live in a state of gratitude and give thanks, the more you'll soon possess to be thankful for.

Step Four

Decide to live in the now. Know that God is now.

Don't look to the past, nor the future. Be with God right now—here, in this time and place. Regrets for the past and worrying about the future will get you nowhere. Tracey and I have been there, and it just doesn't work.

It has been said by many before, but it's worth saying again: You can't change the past. We encourage you to learn from the past, but otherwise it's time to move on.

Now, as far as the future goes, do as the once popular song said: "Don't worry, be happy." Worrying gets you nothing—in fact, it has a paralyzing effect. Tracey and I have been there when we were losing our home. Worrying got us nowhere. What did? *Action.*

Studies show that more than 90 percent of what people worry about never happens. Think about it. What have you worried about that never happened?

Knowing the history of your particular religion is important, but don't become so caught up with the historical aspects of your faith that you miss the fact that God is with you *right here, right now!*

Tracey and I have read the Old and New Testaments, and they've been a great source of inspiration. But to be frank, memorizing and then quoting chapter and verse, has never been a strength for either of us. Because memorization is difficult for us, it depersonalizes our relationship with God and puts God in the past. If you want to tap into the power of God, which is the purpose of this book and the 7 Great Prayers, you must recognize that God is now!

As with the past, the same holds true for the future. Stop thinking about it. Do what's right for *now*. Living every day in a way that strengthens your connection with God and honors God is the best way to prepare yourself for a better tomorrow.

The best role models for tapping into the power of God now are prophets and other spiritual people, be they Martin Luther King Jr., Gandhi, Mother Theresa, or others. They tapped into the power of God in the moment—in the now!

Grasp this one step. Know that God is *always* with you—ready to be your friend, ready to listen, ready to help—and you'll be well on your way to the hopeful and blessed life you desire.

Step Five

Ask with faith. Know that God will answer your prayers . . . in God's time.

It's okay to ask God for help. God is on your side. Or, as Abraham Lincoln said, you are on God's side.

If you want something good and proper, so does God. Ask with faith. Believe with all your heart, mind, and soul that your prayers will be answered. However, realize that you may think you know what you want, but something better may be in store for you. Be open to and aware of the multiple ways that God may answer your prayers.

Give God time to bless you. The blessings will come. Just as an apple tree does not sprout up overnight to give apples the next day, so it is with you and your prayer requests. Give your prayers sunshine (focus on them) and water (give thanks for what you have already received from God), and in God's time your prayers will come to fruition and you will receive your blessings.

Step Six

Be on the alert. Keep your eyes and ears open. Be receptive and watch for signs from God.

There's an expression that "there's no such thing as a co-incidence," and there isn't. What you might think is a coincidence is God at work.

If you have a hunch and a good feeling, have faith that it's God talking with you, and make certain you take action on your hunch. It will lead you toward the blessings you desire.

How do you stay alert? How do you keep your eyes and ears open? You have to maintain a constant dialogue with God, and an easy way to do this is to talk with God using the 7 Great Prayers.

Step Seven

Bless others. Give and you will receive.

So much of living an abundant and blessed life has to do with attitude and your "vibration." This is where the expression "I'm getting bad vibes," comes from. You are a vibrational being.

More often than not, you'll hear someone say that they are getting bad vibes more than good vibes. This is because we are hardwired to recognize danger. This instinct goes back thousands of years—it used to keep man away from danger, such as a hungry predator.

Now these predators have been replaced by people

who may be looking out for their best interests, not yours. The point is, if you get a bad feeling, it's God's way of warning you. Take heed and avoid the danger.

The same goes with goose bumps. Have you ever had a thought or been in a situation where you got goose bumps, that rough, prickly sensation on your skin? If so, it's God again, talking with you, telling you that all is okay, all is good.

You'll learn more about vibrations and God as you read, but for now, know that you are a vibrational being. You have a soul and are connected with God.

Since we all have souls and are connected with God, it makes great sense to bless others and help others. This gets energy and God working for you. Give and you will receive. Give bad, and you'll get bad. Give good, and you'll get good. This is one of God's natural laws: Give and you shall receive.

To attract positive things in your life, you must think and act positively. In addition to living in a state of gratitude all the time, you will want to bless others. You bless others by your thoughts and actions. Do this all day. When you see people, family, friends, coworkers, and strangers, silently and quickly say to yourself, "God bless that person." I must do this a hundred times a day. It takes seconds to say this prayer, and the positive returns I receive are overwhelming.

Feel free to say this quick blessing prayer out loud if it's appropriate. Think, talk, and be active in your blessings and you will attract blessings in your life. It really is that simple!

The Last Step

Now that you know how to attract God's blessings, the simplest and most powerful way to change your life is to say the 7 Great Prayers every day, throughout each day. You can say the entire 7 Great Prayers in just a few minutes, so there's no reason why you can't say them at least ten times a day.

You don't have to say them in sequence, nor do you have to say them all at the same time. Just pray them whenever it makes the most sense—and as with thousands of corn kernels planted in the field, soon you'll be harvesting happiness, health, and wealth!

5

The Power of the
7 Great Prayers

The upcoming chapters will focus on the 7 Great Prayers themselves. Each prayer is accompanied by explanations of why the prayer will help you achieve a closer relationship with God and tap into God's power to reach any goal you desire.

As you read each chapter, I encourage you to use the 21-Day Prayer Journal in Part Four and create customized affirmative prayers. The 7 Great Prayers take on even greater power when you take each prayer and compose individual prayers specific to your needs.

An Example: Getting a New Job

The Fourth Great Prayer is "God, bless me." Now use this foundation prayer to make your own customized Great Prayer, for example:

> God, bless me with a new job that I love.
> God, bless me with a positive attitude to take the
>   right action to look for a job.

The Second Great Prayer is "Thank you God." Now use this foundation prayer to create a Great Prayer that is specific to getting this new job, such as

> Thank you God for attracting the right thoughts and
>   people into my life that got me this new job.
> Thank you God for giving me the motivation to
>   succeed.

Note that this prayer says "this new job." A useful prayer technique is to pray, think, and talk as though whatever blessing you desire has already been received.

In addition to making your own customized Great Prayers, create your own customized affirmations:

> Day by day, in every way, I am getting closer and
>   closer to finding a new job.
> I love my new job. It gives me great happiness.

I take all the appropriate steps to gain employment as
soon as possible.

I am so happy and grateful now that I have found the
perfect job for me.

These examples relate to finding a new job. You'll soon
learn how to use the 7 Great Prayers and prayer techniques as the foundation for achieving whatever goal you
desire: wealth, health, better relationships with family,
friends, and God.

FOR A PRAYER to be truly effective, you must believe in
it, and it should have a profound emotional effect on
you. Remember: "All things are possible to those who believe them."

You must believe in the power of your prayer and that
your desired outcome is truly possible. This is very important; otherwise your prayers will not work.

Believe in yourself.

Believe in God.

What You Want Has to Be Believable

Your mind is extremely powerful *and* programmable. To
attain as much success as possible using this program,
it's important that your mind *believes* that what you're

praying for is attainable. It's all right to have lofty goals though—the higher the better.

Still, just like getting to the top of a tall building when you take the stairs, it's important that you go one step at a time. You can't imagine yourself going up ten flights of stairs in one giant step, but you can imagine going up all ten flights if you were to take one step at a time.

When using the 7 Great Prayers, believe that they will work. Believe in yourself. Believe in God. Believe that you can tap into God's power. Then work your way toward your goal, gradually and persistently.

The Power of Emotion

It's critical that you fully "emotionalize" your prayers. You need to feel your prayers, as well as read and speak them. Yes, *speak*. Whenever possible, say your prayers out loud.

Read your prayers. Speak your prayers. Write your prayers. The more senses you get involved with your prayers, the better!

Tap into Your Subconscious Mind

Your mind has two parts; the conscious and the subconscious. The subconscious mind is the part that operates beneath your conscious mind.

For example, while taking a long car trip, have you ever driven lost in thought, and don't even remember the act of turning the steering wheel and pressing on the gas and brake pedals? How did you drive that long distance without consciously thinking about it? It was your subconscious mind at work. The same part of your mind helps your nervous system breathe, blink your eyes, and digest your food. Your subconscious mind is powerful!

Your subconscious mind is closely connected with God. You want to do whatever you can to keep your subconscious mind in a positive state.

One of the unique features of your subconscious mind is that it believes whatever you tell it, whether or not what you are telling it is true or false. So you want to be careful to make sure that you think, talk, and act positively so you can harness the extraordinary power of your subconscious mind.

You'll notice that most of the prayers in this book are composed in the present tense. When your prayers are stated in the present tense, your subconscious mind will believe that you already are what you are praying to be.

Since your subconscious mind already believes what you are praying for, it will assist you in actualizing your goals with the help of God.

Tap into the Power of "I Am"

You will also see and hear that many of the affirmation prayers in this book contain the words *I am*. These are two of the most powerful words in your vocabulary, especially when used in praying.

Again, you are what you believe. Therefore, when you pray with the words *I am*, you will soon be what you believe—whether it is healthier, wealthier, happier, or closer to God. For example, your affirmation prayers might say:

I am happy, healthy, and wealthy.
I am closer to God.
I am a success.

And to repeat, always pray in the positive sense. Don't pray negatively. For example, you don't want to say, "God, help me not to eat sweets today." Instead, you want to pray:

God, thank you for keeping me free from sweets today.

You won't want to say: "God, help me not to get angry." Instead, you want to pray:

God, thank you for keeping me happy and positive.

Now that you are getting a better understanding of the 7 Great Prayers and how to use them, let's turn the page to the next chapter and learn about tapping into the power of writing your prayers.

6

The Power of Writing
Your Prayers

As you just learned, one of the most powerful ways you can bring God into your life is to solicit the help of your subconscious mind. So say the 7 Great Prayers out loud every day. Say all the affirmation prayers in Part Five out loud, too. Saying the prayers out loud anchors these prayers into your subconscious mind.

Then to really *supercharge* your praying, write each of the 7 Great Prayers ten times. Do this daily, using the 21-Day Prayer Journal in Part Four. Writing your prayers takes your praying to the next level. Then, using the 7

Great Prayers as your foundation, craft your own prayers to meet your personal goals.

The following is an example of how you can use your prayer journal and tailor the 7 Great Prayers to achieve a blessing or goal you desire. For this example, someone wants to increase his or her income:

I love you God (the First Great Prayer).

Thank you God (the Second Great Prayer) for all you've already blessed me with and continue to bless me with.

God, you are within me (the Third Great Prayer). I ask that you give me comfort and strength.

God, bless me (the Fourth Great Prayer) with additional income. Bless me with ideas, people, and events that will give me this additional income. I have this income. It is here now, and it feels great! Thank you God (the Second Great Prayer).

God, I see you everywhere (the Fifth Great Prayer). I see you in myself, I see you in all people, I see you in nature.

God bless and I love (the Sixth Great Prayer) those people who are helping me with this additional income.

God, help me help you (the Seventh Great Prayer). I am using this additional income to provide for myself and for those I love. The work I do helps others, and I am doing everything in my power to help make the world a better place.

As you can see, this example incorporates all 7 Great Prayers.

The Sense of Touch

When writing your prayers, you bring the sense of touch into your praying. Since you are writing, not only will you be visualizing your prayer, you'll also be feeling your prayer.

Traditional prayer is said either internally to oneself or out loud, and many traditional prayers are memorized prayers, written by someone else. The 7 Great Prayers and the customized affirmation prayers you create are *your* prayers. They are prayers said as if you are talking with a friend. And you *are* talking to a friend, your best friend—God.

One of the key benefits to writing your prayers is that to do so you have to focus. So slow down. Stop whatever else you're doing, and focus on the task at hand, which is to write. This is the origin of the expression, "If you want to remember something, write it down." This is also why students take notes from the books they are reading when they are studying. The act of writing connects the wiring in your brain that will help you remember what you've written down.

I hope you are now underlining, using asterisks, and taking notes in the margins of this book as suggested earlier. If not, please start doing so now.

Three Out of Five

The more of your senses you involve in the process of praying, the better. We have five senses: sight, hearing, touch, taste, and smell.

As for the 7 Great Prayers, we see the prayers as we read them, we hear them as we say them out loud, and we touch them as we write out our prayers. By adding the third sense of touch, you are more deeply involved in praying.

More than ever, this writing of your prayers brings in your emotions, which are also critical for effective prayer. So, whatever you do—and we can't say this enough—please don't skip writing your prayers. Use the 21-Day Prayer Journal in Part Four. Should you need additional journals, please visit our Web site at www.the7great prayers.com.

7

The Power of 21 Days

For the 7 Great Prayers to have a true effect on your life, it's critical that you say and use them for 21 days straight. Write the 7 Great Prayers on an index card and carry the card with you at all times. (You can copy the prayer card in this book.)

Read, write, and pray the prayers for 21 consecutive days. If you get to day 12 and stop, you have to start over at day 1. Stick to it, and you'll be on your way to incredible blessings in your life!

Why 21 Days?

Research has proven that it takes 21 days of an activity to create a habit. This 21-day habit rule applies for good and bad habits. Smoke cigarettes for 21 days straight, and you are pretty much guaranteed to be hooked. If you are going to start an exercise program, the best way to make it a lifelong habit is to start by committing yourself to 21 straight days of some form of exercise.

We're convinced that the main reason people fail in getting their prayers answered is because they fail to continue. Don't quit. "Winners never quit, and quitters never win."

Praying should be a lifetime habit—pray without ceasing. This means without ceasing for an hour, a day, a week, a month, or a year.

Our 21-Day Prayer Challenge to You

What's the best way to ensure that you pray the 7 Great Prayers every day? How about a challenge? Tracey and I challenge you to pray the 7 Great Prayers every day for 21 days, starting right after you read the next chapter, which is the First Great Prayer. When you finish reading the next chapter, turn to the 21-Day Prayer Challenge in Part Four.

You do not have to finish reading this book to start the challenge. In fact, we encourage you to take the 21-Day Prayer Challenge while reading.

If you have the companion CD, consider listening to it for 21 days straight as well. Then, after the 21 days, listen to the CD anytime you want to remind yourself of your relationship with God. Tracey and I have been using our CDs for years. We keep a set in our cars and have uploaded the prayers to our iPods, so we listen to the prayers when walking or exercising and right before we go to bed.

As for the 7 Great Prayers themselves, they are designed and written in such a manner that you can say them every day. You'll never tire of using them, just as you would never tire of being in the company of your best friend. They are meant to be a companion to you always.

This is what makes the 7 Great Prayers so powerful: You can use them for life!

PART THREE

The 7 Great Prayers

For a Lifetime of Hope and Blessings

1

I Love You God

The First Great Prayer

Each of the 7 Great Prayers is designed to work with the other prayers, so that when you get to the Seventh Great Prayer, you'll be tapping into the full power of all 7 Great Prayers! Before we get to the First Great Prayer, however, let's make sure we're on the same page regarding our definitions of prayer. Prayer is,

- The act of communication with God
- To address God with adoration or thanksgiving

- An earnest request or appeal for God's help

There are other definitions and uses for prayer—for example, asking for the forgiveness of sins—but for the purposes of the 7 Great Prayers and to attract blessings into your life, we are going to focus on the preceding three aspects of prayer.

The Prayers Have No Order

There is no order to effective daily praying. You'll find yourself using and saying the 7 Great Prayers in a variety of sequences. But for the purposes of teaching you the 7 Great Prayers, we will do them in order. Tracey and I have found that the order I'm about to outline is one of our favorites and the one we use most often. With that said, the first order of daily praying is to praise God.

We all have our life challenges. One of the biggest mistakes we make when praying to God is that we ask for God's help in solving our problems without first giving Him praise.

So the first daily prayer we recommend is a prayer where you praise God. By giving God praise first, we take our minds off our problems and shift our focus onto God.

Praise God.

Focus on God's love. Focus on God's goodness. Focus on your oneness with God.

PRAYER TIP

When focusing and praising God, aim your focus *within*, not to the outside. God's spirit lives within us.

God made us in his image and being, so He is within each and every one of us, including you! The same God who was within every great saint and person who has graced this planet is within you! This is great news! Get closer to God. Tap into God's power.

You have the same access to God as a priest, minister, or prophet. So let God into your heart. Feel God's presence in every cell of your body. Talk with God through the power of affirmative prayer. You don't have to look in the heavens or go to church to find God. The spirit of God is within you—right here—right now!

Since God is within you, when you start praying, say "hello" as you would to your best friend, and give God praise.

The First Great Prayer

"I Love You God"

Now please, don't be fooled by this prayer's simplicity. There's power in simplicity.

Water running over a dam is pretty simple. Put a turbine halfway down the dam—as in the Hoover Dam—and you may have enough power to light all of Los Angeles! Nothing complicated about this process, but boy it sure is powerful. The same goes with the First Great Prayer.

What makes this prayer so great?

- It's easy to remember. It's hard to pray without ceasing if you are struggling to memorize a lengthy prayer.
- Telling someone, especially God, that you love him or her is the ultimate form of praise. And *praise* is the first step in effective praying. You can say this

Great Prayer to yourself all day long, while you eat, walk, drive, work, stand in line at the grocery store, anywhere you go.

And remember, as you say this prayer, focus on God who is within you—not outside, but *within*.

A Quick Story from Tracey

Out of money! How could that be?

Our beautiful home, in a quaint New England town with peach and apple trees, was now up for sale. This home, where we experienced so much joy and laughter, had turned into a place where I cried and worried every day. I worried about where our family would live next. How would we send our children to college? How would we pay the bills? I was gripped with fear and worry. I was depressed, alone, and isolated.

The bottom had dropped out. The McManus family was in an economic crisis.

As I write this story, a few years have passed since we lost everything, including our home. Time heals, love heals, and God heals.

Today I took my morning walk. I smelled the lilacs. I listened to the beautiful songs of birds as they welcomed the new day. I admired the blue of the morning sky—I love every aspect of living in this little New England town where Paul and I raised our three children. As I walked, I thanked God for being so blessed!

Who would have thought?

Just a few years earlier I thought I would never be happy again here or anywhere. Now don't get me wrong. Although I'm happy now, it's taken a lot of hard work, a stiff upper lip, love, and God's help. It's tough on you, your husband, and your kids when you lose your home—not once but twice!

We live in a society where your home, the cars you drive and the clothes you wear are scrutinized under the watchful eye of your so-called friends and neighbors.

But when you have no money, you realize that material possessions aren't the important things in life. Why is it that we have to lose everything to know that having "stuff" doesn't matter? I don't know the answer. But I do know that the real treasures in life are not material but spiritual, such as *love*. Love of God, family, friends, and neighbors. My treasures are Paul, my three children, my extended family, my pets, and my health.

Just as love is the first of the 7 Great Prayers, love and gratitude are the places to start on the path to changing your life for the better. Through the hardship of losing our home, I found that things got better when I focused on gratitude and love. I suggest that you do the same.

Living in a state of gratitude changes the way you see everything. You realize that there are so many things to be thankful for every day. Notice them and be thankful! When you are thankful, your heart is open to love. Celebrate the love of family, friends and God!

OTHER VARIATIONS of the First Great Prayer are:

God, you dwell within me. I love you!
God, you are good and powerful. I love you!
God, you love me, and I love you!

Be creative and make up your own mini prayers. Keep all your prayers short and simple and centered on the First Great Prayer: "I love you God."

Start saying this prayer now. Say it multiple times while drifting off to sleep. Write this prayer and your own variations on a piece of paper and carry it with you at all times. Write it in your prayer journal.

The First Great Prayer

I Love You God

THE 7 GREAT Prayers

The First Great Prayer:
"I LOVE YOU GOD."
Give God praise, take your mind off your life's
challenges, and shift your focus toward God,
good thoughts, and receiving blessings.

The Second Great Prayer:
"THANK YOU GOD."
Take a moment to reflect on all the good things
in your life and give God thanks for them.
Put yourself in a state of gratitude.

The Third Great Prayer:
"GOD, YOU ARE WITHIN ME."
Feel God's presence and know that God is
with you right now.

Make a copy of both sides of this card and tape them together
to create your own prayer card. Make a few extra and give
them to your family and friends.

The Fourth Great Prayer:
"GOD, BLESS ME."
God wants the best for you, so "ask, believe,
and ye shall receive."

The Fifth Great Prayer:
"GOD, I SEE YOU EVERYWHERE."
Connect with God. See the love of God in family,
friends, everyone you meet and in nature.

The Sixth Great Prayer:
"GOD BLESS AND I LOVE ..."
Pray for others that they too receive God's love
and blessings.

The Seventh Great Prayer:
"GOD, HELP ME HELP YOU."
Ask for God's continued strength to fulfill your
life's purpose.

www.the7greatprayers.com

PRAYER ADVICE

During the 21-Day Prayer Challenge, we recommend that you carry this book with you throughout the day. For those times when you don't have this book with you, make a copy of the 7 Great Prayers card and carry the card with you at all times. It will help you learn the 7 Great Prayers and internalize them into your daily prayer life.

Do carry the prayer card with you for 21 consecutive days as you do your 21-Day Prayer Challenge.

Start the 21-Day Challenge Now

The 21-Day Prayer Challenge works best when you take the challenge *while* reading this book and not after you read it. Now that you've learned the First Great Prayer, you are ready to start your prayer challenge. Before you read the next chapter, please turn to Part Four. Read how the challenge works, commit to doing the challenge, and then complete Day 1 of the prayer challenge.

2

Thank You God

The Second Great Prayer

Next we're going to add the Second Great Prayer to your daily praying. The more you pray, the sooner you'll start living a hopeful and blessed life!

First you praise God: "I Love You God" (the First Great Prayer). Next we want to thank God for His many daily blessings, and we do that with the Second Great Prayer.

The Second Great Prayer

"Thank You God"

When times are difficult, whether financially, physically, or emotionally, it can be pretty darn tough to give thanks to God. But you can do it, and you have to do so.

A Quick Story from Paul

When I was seven years old, I was running through the woods in my hometown of Ridgefield, Connecticut, playing with my friends. We decided to have a race to my friend's backyard, which bordered the woods.

Off we went.

I tripped, fell, and landed face first onto a stick that blinded my right eye.

This was a traumatic event for my parents and me. But right from the start, my dad—a man of great faith—was thanking God. Thanking God that it was only one eye. Thanking Him that something worse didn't happen. Thanking Him for the strength that God gave us through this trying time.

My dad got me into one of the best eye hospitals in the world: the Columbia University Presbyterian Eye Hospital in New York City. I had five operations to correct the injury. None of them worked. I had to go into the hospital for weeks at a time. I was on the children's floor, where all of us had various eye problems.

Boy, was I giving God thanks then when I saw little boys and girls, all of whom were worse off than I. Many were blind in both eyes!

While at the hospital I became friends with a boy about my age. His name was Arnold. His parents had brought him all the way to New York from Iowa. I still remember the day when my dad took my hand and, with tears in his eyes, said, "Paul, I just found out that Arnold has brain cancer, and it's terminal."

"What's cancer?" I asked. "What does terminal mean?" My dad explained, and we both cried. Sobbing, my dad held me close, and he gave thanks to God for my health. Then my dad led us in prayer for Arnold and his family.

The Glass Is Half Full

That day—that experience of losing my eye, and then being on a hospital floor with children who were worse off than me, some who were dying—taught me perhaps the most valuable lesson I've learned in my life. Don't focus on the negative; focus on the positive, and *always* give thanks for the blessings you have.

To this day, all I need to do is close my left eye—my good eye—to remind myself that when I try to look out of my right eye, I'm blind. The second I close my good eye, I start thanking God for the fact that I have it. I open my good eye and look around and see my family, friends, and nature, all of which are so beautiful!

Over my lifetime, I've had challenges involving finances, relationships with family and friends, and more. And the tougher the times, the more I continually thank God for all that He's given me and continues to give me.

By thanking God continuously, you open yourself to better receive blessings from God.

Start Praying and Living in Gratitude

Whatever your challenge may be, whether it's related to health, wealth, or happiness, the starting point to turning things around is recognizing that God dwells within. Next you want to give God praise (the First Great Prayer), then give God thanks for the blessings you have already received (the Second Great Prayer), and lastly, start living your life in a state of thanks and gratitude.

So turn your focus off your problems. Praise God and give Him thanks! You really do have so much to be thankful for. Be thankful that you're alive. Be thankful that you have God as your best friend. Be thankful that you're not worse off—regrettably millions of people on this big planet of ours have it worse than you.

Take a moment, right now, and write a list of all that you have to be thankful for. The more you thank God for what you've already received and continue to receive, the more blessings you will receive! Your prayers should be positive, and go something like this:

Thank you God for (fill in the blank).

The Second Great Prayer

Thank You God

PRAYER RECAP

The First Great Prayer
"I Love You God"

The Second Great Prayer
"Thank You God"

Make a list of at least ten prayers of thanks and add them to your daily praying! Write them here:

_____

_____

_____

_____

_____

_____

_____

_____

_____

_____

3

God, You Are within Me

The Third Great Prayer

The Third Great Prayer is one of our favorite prayers. It's empowering to know and feel that God is with you and within you right now!

Yes, God is with you at *all times*. God never leaves you for one second. Right now, while you are reading these words, in this exact moment, God is within you. Stop. Take a moment and feel God's presence and love.

Stop reading. Close your eyes. Bask in God's presence and love. Doesn't this feel great?

Now say the Third Great Prayer with the following affirmations:

God, you are within me and with me right now and you give me comfort. You give me peace. You give me strength. You give me all the blessings I need to live an abundant and blessed life.

A Quick Story from Tracey

Where does inner strength come from? How much can one endure?

Everyone has challenges in life at various times: job, money, health, family, divorce, death of loved ones and more. For us, our biggest life challenge has been money.

Here's an entry in my journal from March 5, 2002:

Paul wrote this e-mail to me and I decided to add it to my journal: "It's at one's lowest moments that man reaches down deep to create his greatest achievements."

Well, I think we've reached our lowest moment today. Kevin, while being dropped off at school today, asked Paul, "Daddy, are we broke?"

Then tonight when Kevin was being put to bed, he said, "Daddy, I look forward to us having money again." "Me too, Kevin," Paul replied. "Thanks for believing in me." "I'll always believe in you, Dad," Kevin said.

We are at our lowest moment today, so I pray that Paul reaches deep to create a great achievement.

Paul hadn't received payment for a job he did, so we can't pay our bills. We have no cash. We are down to one roll of toilet paper in the house. Paul bought food on our gas station credit card, so we have food for two more days. Creditors are calling us. I haven't gone grocery shopping in two weeks other than to buy milk and juice. I could panic, but I laughed. Then Paul just called me and told me the check wasn't coming, so then I cried.

Fast forward to Fall of 2008. How did we make it out of the dark days of March 2002 to days of blessing and abundance now? There's only one answer: *God within!*

I'm reminded of the famous poem, "Footprints in the Sand," in which a man dreamt that he was walking along the beach with God. Across the sky flashed various scenes from his life. He noticed two sets of footprints in the sand, one belonging to him, the other to God. When the last scene of his life flashed before him, he looked back at the footprints in the sand.

He noticed that many times along the path of his life, at the very lowest and saddest points, there was only one set of footprints. This bothered him, so he asked God why God left him when he needed Him most. God replied, "I didn't leave you; it was then that I carried you."

If by chance you are at a low point in your life, I encourage you to turn to God within. Trust and believe that it can and will be okay.

I would also like to give tribute to our three children, Casey, Kevin, and Katherine. They are Paul and my heroes. Through all the difficult times, they never gave up on Paul and me. They never said, why us, why me? When other kids got new clothes and took nice vacations, they never complained.

In hindsight they've been blessed, and they are a blessing to Paul and me. We love each of our children so much! They are better people because of the times we've gone through. They understand the value of work and of money. They understand that what really counts in life are relationships and helping and loving people.

So if you're having a challenge right now as you read this, know that Paul and I are sending our prayers and love to you. We hope that you will find God within. We care, and we pray that you too will turn back years from now to find the hidden blessings in your current challenge.

Setting the Stage for Blessings

The Third Great Prayer is an important building block in setting the foundation for the Fourth Great Prayer, the prayer that will help you attract blessings into your life.

The way to happiness, love, money, health, healing, and more will come from God when you pray the Fourth Great Prayer.

We must first comprehend and use the Third Great Prayer. This amazing prayer calls upon the incredible power of God and makes possible living a life full of abundance and blessings.

The Third Great Prayer

"God, You Are within Me"

Now that we've shared with you the Third Great Prayer, we would like to review how each Great Prayer works.

The First Great Prayer is "I LOVE YOU GOD." It can be a variation of that, such as, "I love you God, and you love me." This first prayer praises God.

The Second Great Prayer is "THANK YOU GOD." This prayer thanks God for the many blessings He bestows on you daily!

The Third Great Prayer is "GOD, YOU ARE WITHIN ME."

Are You Praying Daily?

You most likely won't read this book all in one sitting. It might take a few days, or perhaps a couple of weeks. It all depends on how fast you read and what else is going on in your life.

However, please don't wait until you finish the book to start using the 7 Great Prayers or taking the 21-Day Prayer Challenge in Part Four. The way this book has been written, and the way this prayer program works best, is to start praying the 7 Great Prayers as you learn them. So, please pray the first three Great Prayers today, without ceasing! Remember, a big part of what makes the 7 Great Prayers so special is that they are brief and accessible to all.

They are also powerful because they are easy to remember and to repeat. No wasted words here.

When you pray these three Great Prayers and add to them the next four prayers, you will get closer to God and will be putting yourself on the path to blessings.

You should already have in your pocket or purse a piece of paper with the first two Great Prayers, or you've made a copy of the prayer card in the chapter about the First Great Prayer. If you are writing your prayers on a piece of paper, please get this piece of paper right now and add the Third Great Prayer to it.

No procrastinating. Stop reading. Do it now!

Now that you've added the Third Great Prayer, carry this piece of paper around with you all day long. (Tracey and I carry the prayer card with us always! I also have the prayers along with affirmation prayers written on a piece of paper.)

Remember, you can make slight variations to each of the first three Great Prayers to create your own prayers, and we encourage you to do so.

God Is Not in the Clouds

I don't know about you, but when I was a kid and went to Sunday school, many of the religious books had pictures of God with a white beard, living in the clouds. The image of God that still sticks in my mind is Michelangelo's famous painting on the ceiling of the Sistine Chapel. The painting is called *The Creation of Adam* and shows God—with a white beard and robe—there in the clouds, reaching out with his index finger and touching Adam's finger.

Child psychologists tell us that we are highly impressionable when we are young. My guess is that you're like us, and when people say God's name this image or something similar pops into your mind.

What do you think is more empowering: an image of God far, far away, somewhere in the clouds, or right next to you, dwelling within you?

Knowing where God dwells is vitally important for you to live a hopeful and blessed life, so we're going to continue exploring this topic a little further.

Remember what we learned already in this book:

The spirit of God dwelleth within you
He dwelleth in you, and you in Him

To fully benefit from the 7 Great Prayers, you have to know and feel that God is within you right now, ready to help you, no matter what your challenge may be.

Here are some powerful affirmation add-ons for the Third Great Prayer:

God I believe you are always with me; I feel your presence!
God, you are with me right now; you attract good things to me as you fulfill your purpose through me.

God Is Your Best Friend

How do friends become best friends? It all starts with sharing experiences. The more experiences you share with another person and the more things you have in common, the more the both of you have to talk about. You share the good times, bad times, and tough times.

So, who has never left your side? Never, since the day you were born? Yes, the obvious answer is God.

But the sad thing is that sometimes during the most trying of times—and we know from personal experience—we forget that God is with us right now. Ready to help. Ready to give comfort. Ready to give strength. Ready to give blessings.

Well, no more of that. No more forgetting that God is with you right now, especially when you say the Third Great Prayer!

Let's Review What You've Learned So Far

We're building momentum now for a hopeful and blessed life; we're just four prayers away from the complete collection of the 7 Great Prayers!

Whenever you learn something new, such as the 7 Great Prayers, it's best to add-and-review each step along the way. So, let's add the Third Great Prayer to the first two Great Prayers and review:

PLEASE SAY THE PRAYERS silently to yourself and then out loud, right now. We also encourage you to write your prayers in your prayer journal. Add to and modify the following prayer as you deem appropriate. Do a couple variations. For inspiration, check out Part Five, which contains the 7 Great Prayers and affirmation prayers.

I Love You God.

For the Second Great Prayer, say it out loud, or make a list with at least three prayers of thanks, or do both:

Thank You God for (fill in the blank).

And next pray the Third Great Prayer, along with some affirmations. Again, you can find affirmation prayers in Part Five:

God, You Are within Me.

The Third Great Prayer

God, You Are within Me

PRAYER RECAP

The First Great Prayer
"I Love You God"

The Second Great Prayer
"Thank You God"

The Third Great Prayer
"God, You Are within Me"

4

God, Bless Me

The Fourth Great Prayer

This lesson will be your longest. Please take your time reading the entire lesson and do so in one sitting.

The Fourth Great Prayer is the prayer that will help you attract blessings into your life. But before we get to this life-changing prayer, we would first like to spend a moment with you regarding the secret way to pray.

The Secret Method to Praying

First—and we'll keep saying it again and again—the secret to successful praying is to pray without ceasing. And the easiest way to pray without ceasing is to pray simple, short, and powerful affirmation prayers.

In this chapter, we're going to learn more about the power of affirmations. When you mix affirmations with prayers, the results are dramatic!

Remember, an affirmation is a statement said in the personal, positive, and present tense. For example:

> I like myself, I like myself, I like myself.
> Day by day, in every way, I'm getting closer and closer to God.

We'll continue mixing in affirmations with the 7 Great Prayers. Blending affirmations with prayers is the *secret method* to a closer relationship with God and the easiest and best way to open yourself to receive more of God's blessings into your life!

Program Yourself for Success

It has been said by psychotherapists that by the time a child is ten years old, he or she has heard the word "no" more than fifty thousand times, and that we all hear the word "no" one hundred times more often than "yes."

This negative programming kills self-esteem, destroys self-confidence, and makes people feel physically ill and mentally depressed.

God wants you to like yourself. God wants you to have self-confidence. God wants you to be happy.

With all the negative input we're receiving from friends, family, coworkers, radio, television, and many other sources, it's up to you to make sure that you program your mind with prayer.

If you haven't done so already, starting today we would like you to mix in affirmations with your daily—and ceaseless—praying. As for the order and content of your prayers, do what is most comfortable for you. It isn't an exact science. The important thing is that you pray with *feeling* and *love*. Here are examples of the sort of affirmations you can include:

God, I believe and know you are always with me.

God, you like me, and I like me.

God, your love shines through me.

God, I love you! And you love me.

Thank you God for (fill in the blank).

I'm happy, healthy, and loving.

Day by day, in every way, I'm getting healthier and healthier.

I feel happy, I feel healthy, I feel terrific!
I like myself, I like myself, I like myself.
Thank you God for (fill in the blank).
Day by day, in every way, I'm getting closer and closer
   to God.
I can do it!
With God dwelling in me; I can do anything.
Day by day, in every way, I'm getting (fill in the
   blank).

You'll notice that some of these affirmations are similar, and that's on purpose. Repetition is okay when saying your prayers, as long as you are focused and infuse emotion into them.

Let's Review

Here's a recap of where we are so far in learning about the 7 Great Prayers for a hopeful and blessed life.

Recognize God and praise God (the First Great Prayer). Love who you are, and know that God loves you too.

Thank God (the Second Great Prayer) and then to yourself or out loud pray affirmations that build up your self-worth. Know and believe that God is taking care of you, has always been taking care of you, and will take care of you. All you have to do is connect with Him. Focus not on what you don't have, but give your attention to what you do have, and give God thanks for it.

Feel God's presence. Know that God is within you, right now (the Third Great Prayer). He's your best friend. Know that God is always with you to comfort you, give you strength, and bless you and yours.

Now that we've discussed the power of affirmations and summarized, let's get to the Fourth Great Prayer.

The Fourth Great Prayer

"God, Bless Me"

Think of yourself as a magnet. The things that give you power are your thoughts and prayers. Since we've just learned that we are surrounded by negative versus positive thoughts by a 10-to-1 ratio, it's only natural that you feel negative. This is not good.

Negative thoughts and negative thinking attract negative people, events, and circumstances into your life. This is where the 7 Great Prayers and affirmations come to the rescue.

The 7 Great Prayers, with positive affirmations, help turn you from negative to positive. God is good—100 percent positive! So the more you connect with God, talk with God, and feel God's presence, the more you will magnetize your entire being into one that attracts happiness, health, wealth, and the good blessings you desire.

The Power of Repetition

As we've learned in our prior lessons, it's not a matter of how long or poetic your prayers are to God. It's more important that you keep your prayers personal and powerful. We also learned that the most important thing in praying is repetition, and the easiest way to repeat and memorize a prayer is to keep it short and simple.

With the Fourth Great Prayer, you need to pray for what you want to bring into your life, and do so repeatedly. Take control of your thoughts. Every time you have a negative thought, say to yourself, "switch and replace."

Switch and replace this negative thought with an "I attract" prayer. Triple the time you used to spend in negative thought with positive prayers and affirmations.

For example, let's say you have lost your job and are worried about all the overdue bills. These negative thoughts are filling your mind and stressing you out. To change your negative thinking, you would say the Fourth Great Prayer while mixing in the prior three Great Prayers as follows:

> I love you God. Thank you for all that you've blessed me with already. I know you are always with me and that you are my best friend. You care for me. With your help and goodness, I attract the money I need.
>
> God, you are within me right now and you give me the power to take action to improve my financial situation. Day by day, in every way, my financial situation is getting better and better. With your help I am attracting the right people, events, and circumstances that will improve my finances.
>
> God, I believe in you. I have faith that things are already getting better, and all is well.

Then add the Fourth Great Prayer:

God, Bless Me with (fill in the blank).

Talk with God

Please note how in the preceding prayer we took a string of short affirmative prayers, mixed in the first three of the 7 Great Prayers, and then asked for a particular blessing, creating a customized and personalized prayer. There is no set formula. You can use any number of Great Prayers and affirmations when talking with God.

Also note how informal the prayer is. It is said as though you were talking with your best friend—which you are. You don't want your prayers to be memorized; instead, you want them to be emotional and come from the heart.

You don't give speeches to your best friend. You don't say a memorized prayer. You talk. You talk with emotion, and you talk with passion. Do the same when praying with God.

Note in the preceding sentence that we said *with* God and not *to* God. You don't want to be isolated from God. You want to be connected to God who dwells within you.

If you are going through financial challenges, say the prayer in the preceding section with emotion and with faith, and you'll start to change your mindset from negative to positive in regards to your finances. Following this model prayer, you can customize your prayers for any concern, be it health, relationship, or finding purpose in life.

Gratitude Makes You Positive

Living in a constant state of gratitude changes your being from negative to positive. That's why the Second Great Prayer is so important. Thanking God centers your awareness on what God has already given and continues to give you.

Don't focus on what you lack. Instead, even though you may lack money, good health, a love life, friends, and other things you desire, you cannot think or focus on this lack, as tough as it may seem.

Like a mountain climber, find that nook or cranny that you can employ to make you positive and grab hold as though your life depended on it. Why? Because it does.

No matter how small the blessings you already have in your life, give them your full attention. Give God thanks for them; get into a state of gratitude and stay there.

A Quick Story from Tracey

Like all married couples, Paul and I learn from each other. By our words and actions, we take turns teaching each other how best to live. Probably the number one thing I've learned from Paul about living a hopeful and blessed life is that life is all a matter of how you look at it.

If you look hard enough, or if you look at a situation a different way, you can find blessings. This life skill is especially important when a bad situation arises.

Paul and I are major dog lovers. We have a three-year-old golden retriever named Bailey. She is a love. We also have another dog, Jasper, who is half golden retriever and half basset hound. Jasper, who is adorable, has golden hair like a retriever, barks like a hound dog, and has the short legs of a basset hound. Every time I take a walk with the two dogs, people come up smiling, asking me, "What type of dog is the one with the funny short legs?"

But this story is about Bailey, not Jasper. Ever since Bailey was a puppy, she has had to have something in her mouth. She greets people at the door with her tail wagging and a toy in her mouth.

Bailey discovered at a very young age that socks taste yummy. She not only puts them in her mouth but also eats them. Oh yes, she eats the whole sock! Needless to say, we do our best at the McManus house to make sure no socks are left on the floor.

For those few socks that Bailey has been able to find and eat, she has always been able to pass them through her system. But then there came the time when she found a really big sock.

Paul and I had been watching our expenses and saving every penny we could. We were happy to finally have some money again in a savings account. Really happy! Our plan was to use our savings to buy an older used car for our two oldest children to share. But the universe had another plan for this extra money—Bailey and the big sock.

According to the veterinarian, if Bailey didn't pass the sock, which was lodged in her intestine, she was going to need an expensive operation to have it removed or she would die.

I was freaking out because I didn't want to lose Bailey, who is an important member of our family and a pet we love deeply. I was also very upset because the operation would drain our entire savings. I was in tears. I was looking at this as a no-win situation. Don't have the operation and we lose Bailey. Have the operation and we lose the savings that we worked so hard and long to accumulate.

This is when Paul stepped in and did what he always does. He looked for the good. He looked for the blessing. Sure enough, he found it. Wiping the tears off my cheeks, he said, "Honey, it's okay. Isn't it great that we saved this money? Maybe we've been saving not to buy a used car for the kids but to give Bailey the operation she needs. Thank God we have this money. What would we do if we didn't have this savings?"

Right then and there, with Paul's help, I changed the way I was looking at the situation. We both thanked God for our savings, and Bailey got better.

Paul always has a positive attitude. He also has the ability to turn a negative into a positive, to look at a situation from many angles until he can find the good, the blessing.

Living with Paul, I've learned to always look for the blessing, and this change in my thinking has given me great strength and peace of mind.

Be assured that God will provide you with blessings. He always does. Just know that the blessing you desire may not be the blessing you receive. We wanted a used car for our kids. The blessing we received instead was having the funds necessary to save Bailey's life, which was much more important to us than a used car could ever be.

Do your best to remain positive. Should a bad situation arise, have faith, keep praying, stay positive, and look for God's blessings. They are there waiting for you to discover them.

It's All about Focus

Often we get caught up in the internal soap opera of our own lives. We get so focused on ourselves and our problems, we don't see or thank God for the blessings He gives us daily.

You won't be able to attract God's blessings until you

change your focus. Don't focus on yourself and your problems; instead, focus on God and His love, power, and blessings.

Focus on God, not on yourself and your problems.

Look toward God's goodness and recognize the many blessings you already have in your life and give thanks for what He continues to give you. Please, pause throughout each day to recognize and give thanks to God for the gifts He gives you. Be thankful for the little things, and you will soon be giving thanks to God for the bigger blessings you're asking for.

First give thanks for the little blessings. Thank God for sunshine, the air, your pet, a friend. It's not hard to do. Just look and give thanks. Give thanks for everything!

To be successful in positive prayer, you need to eliminate negative thinking in your life. We know this is extremely hard to do because we struggle with it all the time. Everything will be fine, and then bingo, something bad will happen and instantly we're in a bad mood. So we've found that the best way to break through and switch from negative thinking to a positive life is to pray the 7 Great Prayers, always thinking and visualizing positive outcomes, and to use the power of affirmations.

We're always trying our best to think and pray as though we have already received what we've asked for from God. We ask that you do the same; you'll be amazed at the results!

Don't be ashamed to ask God for blessings. God wants you to ask. Forgive yourself for any sins of your past; God has forgiven you, so forgive yourself. You're a good person and deserve to receive blessings from God.

Live in the now. If something in your past is troubling you, let it go. Do this and you've cleared the way to receive blessings from God.

Knowing that it's okay to ask God for blessings, add the Fourth Prayer to your daily praying and you'll be well on your way to attracting incredible blessings into your life—health, love, money, happiness, purpose, a better relationship with God. To say one of my favorite prayers, begin with the Third Great Prayer:

God, You Are within Me.

Add this affirmation:

I attract God's blessings.

And then add the Fourth Great Prayer:

God, Bless Me.

You can adapt the Fourth Great Prayer to address things you specifically need in your life. As mentioned much earlier, when you ask God for blessings, know what you want and why you want it.

Two Powerful Words

Two of the most powerful words, when used together, are *I am*. When Moses saw the burning bush, he asked, "Who are you?" And the answer Moses received from God was, "I am." So when you use the words *I am*, you are using God's name. *God* and *I am* are one and the same. One more time, we'll go back to what we learned previously:

- The spirit of God dwelleth within you.
- He dwelleth in you, and you in Him.

So here we have it. The understanding about these two powerful words: *I am*. Tap into the power of God and preface your prayer requests with *I am*.

I am also is a must when creating your affirmations. *I am* is personal and positive and said in the present tense.

Here are some examples on how to use *I am* in your prayers:

"I am attracting God's blessings."
"I am happy."
"I am full of life, love, and happiness."
"I am healed."
"I am debt-free."
"I am doing a great job."
"I am connected with God and fulfilling my life's purpose."

Even if you don't feel like you really are any of these statements, say and pray them anyway. As they say in acting school, "Fake it until you make it."

You'll find that when you pray and affirm positive statements like the preceding, and you do it with feeling and enthusiasm, you'll start to receive an avalanche of blessings from God.

Whatever you ask from God, remember the teachings of Jesus:

> *Whatever ye shall ask in prayer,*
> *believing, ye shall receive.*
> —MATT. 21:22

When praying, keep your focus on God "that dwelleth within you." If God dwells in you, and you in Him, it only makes sense that God has the power to attract good things toward Him *and* you, like a magnet attracts iron.

What can make this attraction fail? Negative thinking. A poor attitude. Guilt. Anger. Thinking negative thoughts minimizes and blocks God's ability to attract goodness into your life. Avoid negativity. Forgive yourself. Forgive your spouse. Forgive your enemies. Forgive God. Release the bad and attract God's goodness and blessings right now!

Pray for God's forgiveness, and remember to pray as though you have already received:

Thank you God for already forgiving me.

Don't Say "Please"

For any of your prayers, don't preface them with the word *please*. Doing this presupposes that God may not grant you your blessing. Always pray in the present and positive tense, as though you have already received God's blessing. In doing so, you give Him thanks.

The Fourth Great Prayer

God, Bless Me

PRAYER RECAP

The First Great Prayer
"I Love You God"

The Second Great Prayer
"Thank You God"

The Third Great Prayer
"God, You Are within Me"

The Fourth Great Prayer
"God, Bless Me"

5

God, I See You Everywhere

The Fifth Great Prayer

Knowing that your mind, body, and soul act like a magnet, you'll always want to keep yourself positive—so keep your focus on God, who is good and positive. One of the best ways we've found to keep our focus on God is to pray the Fifth Great Prayer.

The Fifth Great Prayer

"God, I See You Everywhere"

By saying this prayer every day, you will recognize that God, His presence, and His power are everywhere.

If you get caught up in your problems and focus on yourself, you'll miss God's messengers and the events that God has sent your way to help you get the blessing you asked for.

God is always reaching out to help us. But many times He does it in ways we just don't see. By saying the Fifth Great Prayer, you reprogram your internal radio station from WME ("me") to WGOD.

Think about it. A radio can pick up hundreds of different channels, but unless you set the dial to the station playing your favorite song, you'll never hear it.

But when you pray this prayer, "GOD, I SEE YOU EVERYWHERE," you'll be tuning in to God and, in a matter of no time, start receiving blessings in abundance from God.

Here's a well-known and funny story about how God is everywhere, always ready to help, and always sending people or events to help you.

The Big Flood

There was a farmer named Joel whose farm was located on the banks of a river. There came a big flood, and the water around Joel's house was rising steadily. Joel was standing on the porch, watching the water all around him, when a man in a boat came along and called to Joel, "Get in the boat and I'll get you out of here."

Joel replied, "No thanks. God will save me."

Joel went into the house, and the water was starting to pour in. So he went up to the second floor.

As he looked out, another man in a boat came along, and he called to Joel, "Get in the boat and I'll get you out of here."

Again, Joel replied, "No thanks. God will save me."

The water kept rising. So Joel got out onto the roof.

A helicopter flew over, and the pilot called down to Joel, "I'll drop you a rope. Grab onto it and I'll get you out of here."

Again Joel replied, "No thanks. God will save me."

The water rose and rose and soon covered the whole house. Joel fell in the water and drowned.

When he arrived in Heaven, he saw God and asked

Him, "Why didn't you save me from that terrible flood? Did I not show you my faith?"

God replied lovingly, "What more would you have me do? I sent two boats and a helicopter!"

Keep Your Eyes and Ears Open

Recognize that God is everywhere and dwells within everyone (the Third Great Prayer, "God, you are within me") and that God is always working through people to help you, like in the story about Joel.

So pay attention. God wants to help you, and He's reaching out to everyone on this planet, including you, every day. It's your job to keep your eyes and heart open to those people and events God sends your way.

Keeping with the theme of the Fifth Great Prayer, and the mysterious ways in which God works, I'm reminded of Napoleon Hill, the twentieth century's premier success guru, who said, "Within every adversity is the seed of an equal or greater benefit."

What you may think is a problem many times is an opportunity disguised as a problem. So when problems come your way, look and find the benefit that will come to you when you solve the problem. The way you find the benefit is to keep repeating the prayer:

God, I See You Everywhere.

A Quick Story from Tracey

"God, I See You Everywhere" is a prayer close to my heart. I see God in the sun rising in the morning, in the smell in the air on a warm autumn day, in my children and the smiles on their faces.

Seeing God everywhere and thanking God helped me get through our most difficult financial times. What began as a few dark days grew to a string of dismal weeks and months. I was depressed, stressed, and angry, and I couldn't find anything good in the course of the day to think or talk about.

At the lowest point in my depression, I started writing positive thoughts in a journal. This and the 7 Great Prayers helped to turn my life around.

As we were losing our home, juggling bills, and dealing with bill collectors, I would take time out of my day and write down positive things that happened throughout the day along with what I was thankful for.

Sometimes I would stare at a blank journal page for minutes and not write anything. My mind would be racing, thinking about all the negative events that had happened that day. But I wouldn't allow myself to write anything negative in my journal. The page was better off blank than to have something negative written on it.

I would write in my journal about the good health of my family, a great call from my mother, or an amazing hug that I received from one of my children. I'd even note that the deer did not eat my hosta plants the night before. The more I thought about it, the more I realized that the goodness of God is everywhere and there was so much positive going on in my life to be thankful for.

I kept my positive journal in my pocketbook or in the kitchen with me during the day. And when I became depressed, angry, stressed, or sad, I'd pull out my journal and read it. The next thing you know, my attitude would change.

If you're going through difficult times or even if you just want to change your life for the better and be happier, I recommend that you start looking for the goodness in every day. Look for God. Write what you find in a positive journal and then turn to it when you need inspiration.

Once you make a habit of recognizing the blessings all around you, however small they may seem at the time, you will feel better about your life. Your positive journal will be a tremendous resource to you, reminding you to live in a state of thankfulness. You will have a more positive attitude and will connect with God, and this will give you the strength you need to overcome challenges.

A good place to start the habit of positive journaling is by taking the 21-Day Prayer Challenge. Write your positive thoughts in the journal in Part Four. Then, when you complete the 21-Day Prayer challenge, buy a big journal or notebook and keep writing your positive thoughts along with the 7 Great Prayers and affirmation prayers. You too will be on the path to a hopeful and blessed life.

K.I.S.S. (Keep It Sweetly Simple)

We're urging you to stick to the prayers and prayer techniques we've outlined in this book. We highly recommend spending more of your time in prayer. Recall the countless writings of Jesus praying—praying in public, praying with his disciples, praying in private. Pray as Jesus did. He prayed from his heart. He kept his prayers simple and full of love. If you're too busy to memorize a prayer, you're not incorporating your heart and soul into your prayers.

God doesn't want mindless memorization. He wants your full attention and your full heart and soul. The easiest, best, and most powerful way to do this is through short and simple prayers. These prayers can be life-changing if you say them with love in your heart, making them part of your daily life.

Again, we encourage you to write each of the 7 Great Prayers on an index card or use the prayer card and carry it with you at all times. Make copies of the affirmation prayers in Part Five and carry them in your pocket or purse. This book is designed so you can carry it with you and refer to it during the day. Also use the 21-Day Prayer Journal in Part Four.

Please take a moment right now—and we mean right now—pull out your piece of paper or your prayer card, and write down the first five Great Prayers:

I Love You God.
Thank You God.
God, You Are within Me.
God, Bless Me.
God, I See You Everywhere.

The first three prayers build the foundation for the prayer that attracts an abundant life and blessings from God. The Fourth and Fifth Great Prayers enable you to get in tune with God to receive His blessings.

Use the first five Great Prayers as your foundation and template. From this foundation you then make modifications, personalizing each prayer to your needs. For example, create various "Thank you prayers" for the specific blessings you've received from God.

When asking for blessings, always make sure you pray personally and positively as though you've already received the blessing you're praying for.

Add affirmations to your prayers. These affirmations don't have to make any reference to God. They are powerful in their own right. Mix affirmations like the following with the 7 Great Prayers for even more inspiration:

I can do it!

I believe in God, I believe in me.
Day by day in every way I'm getting better and
    better.
I am happy, healthy, and wealthy.

When you say your affirmation prayers, make sure they are said in the present tense, are personal, and are positive.

Walk with God

God made the earth, so go out and enjoy it. Take it all in. In our modern society, we've become detached from nature, and this is unhealthy.

Millions of people wake up to the noise of an alarm clock. While they get ready to leave, they watch the TV morning program. Dash to the car, turn on the radio. Fight traffic to get to work. Spend the day in a cubicle or an office. Drive home. Then sit in front of the TV for a few hours, go to bed, and repeat the process the next day. During the to-and-fro, the only time millions of people are outside is walking from their car to the office, the store, or home. Even though God is within you this whole time, it's almost impossible to connect with God in a routine like that.

May we suggest that you take a walk with God? Now, we're not talking power-walking with God. We mean a nice casual stroll, by yourself or with a loved one, where you just take in the beauty of God's creation.

We live in Connecticut and are blessed with four seasons. I take walks almost every morning with our two dogs, Bailey and Jasper. I walk in a wooded area with trails and am fortunate that I can let the dogs off their leashes. As I walk, I breathe in the crisp air. I look at the crystal blue sky. In spring the trees are budding. In fall the Canadian geese fly overhead on their journey south. Bailey chases squirrels up trees. Butterflies fly. Streams babble.

I walk with God.

I see God everywhere, and I know that God is with me and within me. No matter how stressful the previous day was, or how worried I may be about what lies ahead, this is my time. This is God's time.

I say the 7 Great Prayers. I no longer have to look at a prayer card or piece of paper. Praying the 7 Great Prayers comes as naturally to me as breathing. These morning walks are often the best part of the day for me. It's my time to connect with God. My time to connect to God's power.

No TV. No radio. Just me walking with God.

I do these walks with Tracey, too. Sometimes we talk to each other. Other times we both just talk with God and see God everywhere.

We highly recommend that you take similar walks. Walk and talk with God. When you connect with God's power, stress dissolves and you'll be energized and feel good about yourself. You'll connect with God and receive the comfort, peace, and strength to overcome any challenge you may have in your life.

God dwells within us. God is in nature.

The Fifth Great Prayer

"God, I See You Everywhere

PRAYER RECAP

The First Great Prayer
"I Love You God"

The Second Great Prayer
"Thank You God"

The Third Great Prayer
"God, You Are within Me"

The Fourth Great Prayer
"God, Bless Me"

The Fifth Great Prayer
"God, I See You Everywhere"

6

God Bless and I Love …

The Sixth Great Prayer

By now you should have developed the daily routine of praying the first five Great Prayers every day, all day long. You should also be doing the 21-Day Challenge as outlined in Part Four. How are you doing? What day are you on?

When you pray the Third Great Prayer, it helps you become aware of the awesome power of God that is within you. Again, this prayer is

God, You Are within Me.

With Prayer Four, you learned how to pray to attract God's blessings into your life:

God, Bless Me with (fill in the blank).

The Fifth Great Prayer helps you recognize God's presence everywhere, in everything, and in everyone:

God, I See You Everywhere.

Now that you see God everywhere, I ask that you incorporate the Sixth Great Prayer into your daily prayers.

The Sixth Great Prayer

"God Bless and I Love (fill in the blank)"

Loving one another has always been one of God's top commandments and the teachings of Jesus tell us the same:

Love thy neighbor as you would love yourself.

Now let's keep in mind why you first found our book or Web site. You may have been searching for something on the subject of prayer. If you're like most of the people who purchase *The 7 Great Prayers* or visit our site, you are looking for prayers to attract blessings and abundance into your life.

First, you're not alone. Hundreds and hundreds of great people just like you come to our site each day looking to attract abundance and blessings into their lives. Like those people, you can have abundance and blessings! But nothing is free, and that includes requests to God. To receive, you must give, and the best and easiest thing you can give is your love for God and for others.

Connect with Others and Connect with God

When you open your heart to other people, you are acting and living as God commanded you to do. God will give you the blessings you request only if you are good to yourself and to others.

If God is always with you, that means He is also with everyone you meet: friends, family, coworkers, people on the street, everyone! God is omnipotent.

And yes, God is even with those people you don't like and those who have wronged you. Unlike you, though, they may not recognize that God is within them. For some of these people, you may have to look hard and deep into their souls to find God.

Before we get into connecting with the people who you don't care for or who have wronged you, let's address the easy part and give blessings to all those whom you know and meet.

As for myself, I pray this prayer, all day long:

God Bless and I Love (fill in the blank).

The first people I pray this prayer to are members of my family. When I wake and turn to see my sleeping wife, I say,

God bless and I love you, Tracey.

When I say this prayer to my wife, I look deep into her soul and say it to her and to God who is within her, the same God who is within you and me. I then say this prayer silently or out loud when I see my children.

A Quick Story from Tracey

I loved our children's voices when they were little. The sweet, high-pitched voices of childhood are so innocent. I especially enjoyed Casey's voice. Maybe it was because she is our oldest.

Casey was the first to learn the "God Bless and I Love ..." prayer. I think she was around three years old when she began saying this prayer. And once she learned it, she prayed it every night. She absolutely loved saying it!

As I sat on the edge of little Casey's bed, we started saying the Sixth Great Prayer:

> God bless and I love Mommy, Daddy, Kevin (her baby brother), and Mandy (our dog).

After praying for her immediate family, she continued with her extended family:

> God bless and I love Honey and Pop (my parents).
> God bless and I love Grammy and Grampy (Paul's parents).

Casey would pray, by name, for each of her aunts, uncles, and cousins. She even included all their pets!

After praying the "God Bless and I Love ..." prayer for each of our relatives, she would pray for family that had passed away. Even her fish:

God bless and I love my fish up in heaven.

Nobody was left out. After family, relatives, and all pets were prayed for, Casey then continued praying for all our friends, her friends, and, of course, their pets. She would go on and on and on, blessing and praying for absolutely every person and pet she had ever met in her life. As I tiptoed out of her room, she would continue praying:

God bless and I love ...

Saying the Sixth Great Prayer was quite an event, and I have to admit, I loved every minute of saying this prayer with Casey.

The "God Bless and I Love ..." prayer was the first prayer Casey learned. Now Casey is twenty, and she's still praying this prayer.

If you have children or grandchildren, I suggest you try saying this prayer with them at bedtime. It's a great way to introduce them to the power of prayer, and it's a fantastic way to spend important bonding time with those you love.

How long you say this prayer doesn't matter; what counts is that you and those you love say it daily and with meaning. Praying this prayer before bedtime creates two important lifetime habits:

- Praying before going to sleep, which is probably the best time to pray.
- Praying, blessing, and expressing love for family, friends, and others.

I came up with the Sixth Great Prayer more than seventeen years ago, and it is a lifetime habit. I hope that you'll start saying this Great Prayer every day and night, and that you'll teach it to those you love.

The Power of "I Love You"

Many times after talking to our children, before we hang up the phone or go out the door, we'll say "I love you." It's a great habit to get into, and we encourage you to develop this habit too.

I say "I love you" even if we've had a tough discussion and we're not happy with one another at the moment. I say this powerful statement to both the person and to God, who I know is within him or her.

I even tell my coworkers and people I've been doing business with for some time that I love them; I'll finish the phone call with "Love ya!" I've done this for many years, and why not? This is God's commandment to us. If you love someone, let him or her know it. It's good for them, and it's good for you!

Your spirit is like a flowing river, and the best way you can keep it flowing is by saying and thinking "I love you" all day long. If you don't do this, and you repress this important thought and expression, you act like a dam to the river, backing up all this energy. This is not a good thing. Your love is meant to be shared and to flow; it's not meant to be kept within.

Now, let's return to the lesson and the Sixth Great Prayer. Not only do I use the "GOD BLESS AND I LOVE YOU" prayer with Tracey and our kids, I then say it internally to many of the people I meet during the day.

When picking up my clothes at the dry cleaners, I say it to the cashier. I say it to the toll collector, the bank teller, and the gas station attendant. I say it to anyone and everyone. (I say it not necessarily out loud, but to myself. It's important to be respectful of others.)

When I say it, especially to those I've never met before, I look into their eyes. I look into their soul, knowing that the same God who is within them is within me, and I say it to recognize God and to praise God, as in the First and Third Great Prayers.

Are you starting to see how all 7 Great Prayers work together? Do you see how each prayer adds power to the other prayers? Again, this is why these prayers are so great!

Breaking Down Barriers

Now let's talk about saying the Sixth Great Prayer to those whom you don't like and who may have wronged you. At first I found this tough to do. To be honest, I still have some challenges in doing this, but I know I have to if I'm to be a true child of God, if I'm to do God's work here on this planet, and if I'm to attract blessings and abundance to myself and my family.

So, to those whom you don't like, and to those who have wronged you, still say this prayer. Say it when you see them, when they are not around, and when you think of them. The important thing is to just say it!

God is somewhere within these people, although you may need to look really hard and deeply.

The Power of Forgiveness

It's not healthy to harbor ill feelings towards anyone. A different twist to the Sixth Great Prayer, when it comes to someone you do not like, is to say,

I forgive you and God bless and I love you.

Now you're not acknowledging your love for the wrongdoings of this person. Instead you are showing your love for the goodness within that person, the God within. This prayer accomplishes two things. First, it just may help the person be a better person. Second, it helps you. For you to truly attract more blessings into your life, you have to get in tune with God's positive energy. Forgive and forget. Let go and let God.

With this said, keep yourself and those you love safe. Some people, maybe even family or friends, act in ways that are hurtful. They are negative, and some may want to do you harm. For these people, forgive them and then stay away from them.

As you start incorporating the Sixth Great Prayer into your life, and as you start blessing everyone you meet, you will be positioning yourself to attract blessings from God. For you never know through which person or persons God may work to help you in your life.

The Sixth Great Prayer

God Bless and I Love ...

PRAYER RECAP

The First Great Prayer
"I Love You God"

The Second Great Prayer
"Thank You God"

The Third Great Prayer
"God, You Are within Me"

The Fourth Great Prayer
"God, Bless Me"

The Fifth Great Prayer
"God, I See You Everywhere"

The Sixth Great Prayer
"God Bless and I Love ..."

7

God, Help Me Help You

The Seventh Great Prayer

I hope that after you finish reading this book, you will have a better understanding of the incredible power of prayer. That when you pray by using short, simple, and positive affirmations in the present tense, you truly change your life for the better. You can *attract* blessings into your life.

One last time, praying is not a one-day, one-week, or one-month activity, but a lifelong tool for a better life.

The final Great Prayer puts everything together and completes the cycle. To get you must first give, and it is better to give than to receive.

One of America's foremost philosophers, Ralph Waldo Emerson, said it best in his famous essay "Compensation," when he said that whatever you put out into the universe will come back to you tenfold.

So, if you want love, give love.

If you want financial security, contribute your time to a church or any organization that helps those in need. There was a time in my life that, due to a failed business, I was completely broke. I had no money to give to the church, so I gave with my time. If your back is up against the wall financially, give your time: to the church, to help a friend, to listen to a child. When you have nothing else, you can always give time, which is the most valuable gift you can give anyone.

The Seventh Great Prayer

"God, Help Me Help You"

Many times we wonder, "What am I on earth for?" You're here for one reason, and that's to do good. Look, think, and pray to God for help and guidance on what you should do to help better mother earth and all those who reside on it.

I know that if you're like me, there will be times when you wonder to yourself, "What is this all about? Why am I here?" The answer is, to do good works for God.

Whether you are young or old, you can find some way to help others. Nothing gives you more purpose and joy than helping someone.

So pray the Seventh Great Prayer every day, along with the other Great Prayers. And the more good you do, the more God will send blessings to you. These blessings don't have to be purely financial- or health-related. The blessings can be something as simple as seeing someone smile at you or hearing someone give you a hearty "Thank you" for something you said or did.

One of the easiest yet most resounding things you can do to do God's good work is just recognize someone for their good works. Yes, you should give God praise, but you should also give praise to those around you.

A Quick Story from Tracey

Thanksgiving is one of my favorite holidays!

My maternal grandfather, Willard Pleuthner, was an

extremely loving person and very close to God. His whole life, he lived the Seventh Great Prayer, "God, Help Me Help You."

My grandfather worked in New York City, a short train ride from his home in Scarsdale, New York. Grandpa Pleuthner felt that no one should be alone on Thanksgiving. One year he figured that many people from other countries who were working at or visiting the United Nations were going to spend Thanksgiving alone. So he called the U.N. and extended an invitation to anyone who didn't have a place to go for Thanksgiving to come to his home and celebrate the holiday with him and his family.

So that Thanksgiving Day, Grandpa went and stood in front of the Scarsdale train entrance. Since the foreign guests did not know who he was, he wore a red rose on his lapel, and the group was instructed to gather around the man with the red rose. When they were all assembled, off to my grandfather's home they went.

When the group arrived at his home, family and guests were strangers. Hours later, when the U.N. guests left, everyone was part of one large, loving, international family—God's family.

That first Thanksgiving was such a success, my grandfather made welcoming U.N. staff and visitors into his home to celebrate Thanksgiving a tradition. My mom said she never knew who was going to join them for Thanksgiving, but she did know that whoever came would be interesting and that everyone would have fun. There would be lots of laughter and love at the dining room table.

I've continued my grandfather's Thanksgiving tradition of helping others. In the spirit of the Seventh Great Prayer, "God, Help Me Help You," we've opened our home over the years to those who otherwise would have spent Thanksgiving or Easter alone.

Just as with my grandfather, Paul and I feel great joy inviting into our home people who would otherwise have spent the holiday alone. It feels wonderful helping others!

One special guest has celebrated so many holidays and other important events with us that she has become an important part of our family. We love her, and she loves us. When this friend found out about our financial challenges, she called and said, "Tracey, you've been such a love inviting me into your home all these years. I'm so sad to hear you're having money problems. I want to help you. I think getting a college education is extremely important, so I'm going to pay Casey's tuition this year, okay?"

I was in shock—speechless. Paul and I welcomed this lovely lady into our home for years without ever thinking once about getting anything in return. We were just living the Seventh Great Prayer, "God, Help Me Help You." We found out right then and there that if you're always looking for ways to help others, help will find you when you need it. God will work through others to help you.

We graciously accepted her kind offer. Her help en-
abled Casey to stay in college. They continue to have a
special relationship, and we're forever thankful to our
friend and God for help when we were in need.

"God, Help Me Help You" is a fantastic prayer and
motto to live by—imagine a world in which everyone is
helping others and sharing God's love!

The Seventh Great Prayer

God, Help Me Help You

PRAYER RECAP

The First Great Prayer
"I Love You God"

The Second Great Prayer
"Thank You God"

The Third Great Prayer
"God, You Are within Me"

The Fourth Great Prayer
"God, Bless Me"

The Fifth Great Prayer
"God, I See You Everywhere"

The Sixth Great Prayer
"God Bless and I Love …"

The Seventh Great Prayer
"God, Help Me Help You"

8

Putting It All Together

1. I Love You God.
2. Thank You God.
3. God, You Are within Me.
4. God, Bless Me.
5. God, I See You Everywhere.
6. God Bless and I Love …
7. God, Help Me Help You.

As simple as it may sound, all you have to do to have a life full of abundance and blessings is to use these prayers every day for the rest of your life. Say these prayers to yourself, say them out loud, write them down whenever possible, and live a life of gratitude. Follow the tips and methods outlined in this book and your life will get better. Don't quit. Stick with the 7 Great Prayers and you will be on the path to a hopeful and blessed life. Your life will have purpose. It will be a happy life that both you and God will be proud of.

At the beginning of the book, I asked something of you, and I'll ask again right now. I challenge you to say these prayers for 21 consecutive days. At the end of those 21 days, judge for yourself whether these seven prayers have helped you. As a favor to yourself, as a favor to God, please try this 21-day experiment. I believe you'll be amazed how quickly your life will change for the better. I hope you are already taking the challenge. If not, please turn to Part Four and do so.

It Was a Pleasure Meeting You

Somehow, some way, you were led to this book for a reason. Tracey and I believe you were led here so you could become closer to God and learn how to use God's power for positive life changes.

Throughout this book, we've met and we've connected. It was a pleasure meeting you, and we consider you now a close friend.

It's our goal to share this book and the message of the 7 Great Prayers with millions of people. We believe these seven prayers can help both young and old live a better life. Please join us on this mission. When you have success, send us an e-mail with your success story. We want to hear from you. The more prayer success stories we receive and share with others, the more people we can help get closer to God.

Share your thoughts, comments, and your prayer success stories at the www.the7greatprayers.com/shareyourstory.

God bless you always and may your life be full of blessings!

PART FOUR

The 21-Day
Prayer Challenge

First, we hope that you skipped to this 21-Day Prayer Challenge as we asked you to at the start of the book. If so, we congratulate you! You've made an important step in living closer to God, connecting to God, and tapping into God's power so you can live a more hopeful and blessed life.

Write in This Book

Some people like to write in their books; others do not. As for me, I write in all my books because it helps me focus on what I'm reading. The more active you are in the reading process, the quicker you learn and, most importantly, recall and use what you've learned.

I fondly remember the first day in my freshman English class at Lynchburg College as we started reading Ralph Waldo Emerson's famous essay on "Compensation." As the students in the classroom each read a paragraph, our teacher, in a charming southern accent, yelled out, "I want you underlining, circling words and phrases, and writing in the margin. That book you hold in your hand is not something to be saved in a museum-like fashion; it's for learning, and how do you learn? You write in your book—heck, why not? You paid for the book—so now use it!"

From that day on, I've been writing in all my books, and I can tell you from experience that it works! Not only do I get more out of my reading, I can also flip through the pages of my best books and in seconds I'm reading my favorite passage, complete with my annotations, for reference and inspiration!

Make Copies

Now that I've pontificated about how important it is to write in your book, I am going to ask that you make copies of the following 21-Day Journal.

My suggestion is that you first make a blank master copy set and then file this master set away for future use.

Next, make another set for your personal use. If, as I've recommended, you are reading the 7 Great Prayers with a partner, make an additional set for him or her.

With your master set safely filed away, feel free to start your 21-Day Prayer Challenge using the copy you just made or the journal pages that follow.

If you need 21-Day Journal refills, you can download them at www.the7greatprayers.com/journal.

The Power of 21 Days

Previously we wrote about the power of 21 days, so I won't repeat much of what I've already said. What I will say again is that to create a *lifetime habit,* it takes 21 days of a repeated activity. The 7 Great Prayers are for daily and lifetime use, so you need to make the 7 Great Prayers and affirmation prayers a habit.

Whatever you do, stick to writing your prayers in the journal for 21 days. If you make it to day 6, for example, and then miss a day, back to day 1 you go. No "get out of jail free" card here.

Stick to journaling your prayers for 21 days straight. Do this, and you're well on your way to that hopeful and blessed life.

Blessings I Want and Why I Want Them

Before you start your 21-Day Prayer Challenge, please write down a list of the blessings you want and why you want them. This is critical. Many of us know *what* we want, but *why* we want them is a little cloudy—your mind, and God, work best when you are as specific as possible in your requests. Here are a few examples.

I *want* to be blessed with a job. Here is *why*: Having a job will give me the money required to provide for my family. Having a job will allow me to pay my mortgage or rent. Having a job will increase my self-esteem and I will feel good about myself.

I *want* to be blessed and cured of my health challenge. Here is *why*: When I am healed I will have more energy. When I am healed I will be able to provide for myself and those I love. When I am healed I will be in a position where I can help others.

Be specific and personal when creating your blessing *want* and *why* list. If you run out of space, purchase a spiral notebook and dedicate this notebook entirely to the 7 Great Prayers and your abundant and blessed life prayer program.

_____

_____

_____

_____

_____

_____

_____

_____

_____

_____

_____

_____

_____

_____

_____

_____

_____

_____

_____

_____

_____

_____

_____

_____

_____

_____

_____

_____

_____

_____

_____

_____

_____

_____

_____

_____

_____

_____

_____

21-Day Prayer Journal

Day One   Date: _____

"I Love You God"

Write the preceding prayer a few times along with different ways you praise and love God.

_____

_____

_____

_____

_____

_____

_____

_____

_____

_____

_____

_____

_____

Day Two   Date: _____

"Thank You God"

Write the prayer along with prayers of thanks, detailing the many ways God has blessed and continues to bless you and yours.

_____

_____

_____

_____

_____

_____

_____

_____

_____

_____

_____

_____

_____

_____

Day Three   Date: _____

"God, You Are within Me"

Write this prayer along with prayers that recognize that
God's spirit is always with you.

_____

_____

_____

_____

_____

_____

_____

_____

_____

_____

_____

_____

_____

_____

Day Four   Date: _____

"God, Bless Me"

Personalize and write the blessings you want to receive from God. Write and pray as though you've already received these blessings from God. Believe, with all your heart, and have faith that you've already received these blessings.

_____

_____

_____

_____

_____

_____

_____

_____

_____

_____

_____

_____

Day Five   Date: _____

"God, I See You Everywhere"

Write this prayer recognizing God's loving and omnipotent presence everywhere: in family, friends, coworkers, neighbors, and nature.

_____

_____

_____

_____

_____

_____

_____

_____

_____

_____

_____

_____

_____

Day Six   Date: _____

"God Bless and I Love ..."

Write this prayer and fill in the ending—for example, "God bless and I love my spouse, parents, children, friends, and those in need of blessings."

_____

_____

_____

_____

_____

_____

_____

_____

_____

_____

_____

_____

_____

Day Seven   Date: _____

"God, Help Me Help You"

Ask for God's help and guidance in fulfilling His will and for finding and fulfilling your life's purpose.

_____

_____

_____

_____

_____

_____

_____

_____

_____

_____

_____

_____

_____

_____

_____

Day Eight   Date: _____

"I Love You God"

You are now in your second week of your prayer program. Write the daily prayer and from here on add affirmation prayers and the 7 Great Prayers to your daily
prayer journaling. On the top of each page, we've given
you some affirmative prayer suggestions—write these
prayers along with those that you create. You can find
more affirmative prayers in Part Five.

    I am full of God's love.
    I am happy, healthy, and loving.
    I love the Lord, my God, with all my heart, mind,
        body, and soul.

_____

_____

_____

_____

_____

_____

_____

_____

Day Nine   Date: _____

"Thank You God"

Thank you God for the gifts you give me.
God, you are always with me and you give me peace
    and joy; thank you!
God, you give me power and energy.

_____

_____

_____

_____

_____

_____

_____

_____

_____

_____

_____

_____

_____

Day Ten   Date: _____

"God, You Are within Me"

I pray in earnest and I'm sincere; therefore I can attain
   wonderous results through prayer.
God, when I pray, I fix my attention on your goodness,
   love, and power to remedy any ill I may have.
God, you smiled on me when I was born.

_____

_____

_____

_____

_____

_____

_____

_____

_____

_____

_____

_____

Day Eleven   Date: _____

"God, Bless Me"

I am being led on the right path for me today, leaving all
the details to God.
I am feeling peace in this very moment.
I am terrific just the way I am.

_____

_____

_____

_____

_____

_____

_____

_____

_____

_____

_____

_____

Day Twelve   Date: _____

"God, I See You Everywhere"

I attract love.

I attract good health.

God, I deserve a life full of abundance.

All of God's energies are guiding me to the perfect place
to live, create, and be peaceful.

_____

_____

_____

_____

_____

_____

_____

_____

_____

_____

_____

_____

Day Thirteen   Date: _____

"God Bless and I Love ..."

God bless and I love my friends.
God bless and I love my family.
God bless and I love everyone I meet.

_____

_____

_____

_____

_____

_____

_____

_____

_____

_____

_____

_____

_____

Day Fourteen Date: _____

"God, Help Me Help You"

God, help me to help you and others.
Nice people are helping me.
I turn problems into advantages.

_____

_____

_____

_____

_____

_____

_____

_____

_____

_____

_____

_____

_____

_____

Day Fifteen   Date: _____

"I Love You God"

I am terrific just the way I am.
I believe in God and I believe in myself.
I am happy, healthy, and full of God's love.

_____

_____

_____

_____

_____

_____

_____

_____

_____

_____

_____

_____

_____

Day Sixteen   Date: _____

"Thank You God"

Thank you God for loving me.
I am a loving person.
We love because God first loved us.

_____

_____

_____

_____

_____

_____

_____

_____

_____

_____

_____

_____

_____

Day Seventeen   Date: _____

"God, You Are within Me"

God, you are always within me and you give me
   strength.
God, you are always within me and you give me
   courage.
God, you are always within me and you attract blessings
   to me.

_____

_____

_____

_____

_____

_____

_____

_____

_____

_____

_____

Day Eighteen   Date: _____

"God, Bless Me"

I use prayer to become one with you, God.
I rejoice, I am glad, I give praise, and I give thanks!
I release all negative thoughts about myself and the
   world I live in.

_____

_____

_____

_____

_____

_____

_____

_____

_____

_____

_____

_____

_____

Day Nineteen Date: _____

"God, I See You Everywhere"

God, you and I are best friends.
Thank you God for watching over me.
I attract love, good health, and God's blessings.
I am smart. I am precious. I deserve God's blessings.

_____

_____

_____

_____

_____

_____

_____

_____

_____

_____

_____

_____

_____

Day Twenty   Date: _____

"God Bless and I Love..."

I am letting go of doubt, fear, and distrust, and trusting
   God and quietly accepting the unknown.
God, I love you and I need you; come into my heart and
   bless me, my family, and my friends.

_____

_____

_____

_____

_____

_____

_____

_____

_____

_____

_____

_____

_____

Day Twenty-One   Date: _____

"God, Help Me Help You"

I am a good person; God, you are proud of me.
God, you are always with me and you give me health,
  love, and wealth.
I feel happy, healthy, and terrific!

_____

_____

_____

_____

_____

_____

_____

_____

_____

_____

_____

_____

_____

Prayer Reflections

Write additional notes and prayers here.

_____

_____

_____

_____

_____

_____

_____

_____

_____

_____

_____

_____

_____

_____

_____

_____

_____

Prayer Reflections

Write additional notes and prayers here.

_____

_____

_____

_____

_____

_____

_____

_____

_____

_____

_____

_____

_____

_____

_____

Prayer Reflections

Write additional notes and prayers here.

_____

_____

_____

_____

_____

_____

_____

_____

_____

_____

_____

_____

_____

_____

_____

_____

_____

Prayer Reflections

Write additional notes and prayers here.

_____

_____

_____

_____

_____

_____

_____

_____

_____

_____

_____

_____

_____

_____

_____

_____

_____

PART FIVE

The 7 Great Prayers

with Affirmation Prayers

The First Great Prayer—

I Love You God

Affirmations

I love you God.

Thank you God for loving me.

I give thanks to you God for you are good; your love
    endures forever.

I love you God; you and I are best friends.

I love you God, with all my heart, mind, body, and soul.

God, you are good, loving, and powerful.

God, the earth is full of your unfailing love.

God, I follow the commandment that we love each
    other.

I love my neighbor as I love myself.

God, I am never alone; you surround me with your love.
I do not seek revenge, nor bear a grudge against any of
    God's people; I love my neighbor as I love myself.
Above all, I love my family, friends, and fellow man.
God, I love you and I need you. Come into my heart and
    bless me, my family, my home, and my friends.

My Affirmation Prayers

_____

_____

_____

_____

_____

_____

_____

_____

_____

_____

_____

_____

_____

_____

_____

_____

_____

The Second Great Prayer—

Thank You God

Affirmations

Thank you God.
Thank you God; you give me power and energy.
Thank you God; you give me health.
God, I look for ways to thank you always. I live in a
    constant state of gratitude.
Thank you God for watching over me.
Thank you God for the gifts you give me.
Real help comes from you, God.
With all my might I give thanks up to you, God.
God, thank you for loving me.
I am grateful for what God gives me daily.
God, I thank you in advance for the blessings you give
    me.

My Affirmation Prayers

_____

_____

_____

_____

_____

_____

_____

_____

_____

_____

_____

_____

_____

_____

_____

_____

_____

The Third Great Prayer—

God, You Are within Me

Affirmations

God, you are within me right now.

God, you are within me and you give me strength.

God, you are with me and you give me love.

God, you are with me right now and you give me happiness.

God, you are with me and you attract blessings to yourself and me.

God, you and I are best friends.

I am never alone because you are always with me; this gives me comfort and strength.

Day by day, in every way, I'm getting closer and closer to you, God.

God, you are with me right now, and you give me peace and joy.

God, you are with me right now, and you give me health and wealth.

God, I love you and I need you. You are with me right now. Come into my heart, and bless me, my family, my home, and my friends.

In times of trouble, I call to you and you are with me and answer me.

My Affirmation Prayers

_____

_____

_____

_____

_____

_____

_____

_____

_____

_____

_____

_____

_____

_____

_____

_____

_____

_____

_____

The Fourth Great Prayer—

God, Bless Me

Affirmations

God, I attract your blessings.

When I pray, I fix my attention upon you, God.

God, bless me with the good that I desire.

I fix my attention on your goodness, your love, and your power to bless me.

God, you are with me at all times; you are like a magnet and you attract blessings, in all forms, my way.

God, you are always with me and you give me strength, happiness, and peace.

I am being led on the right path for me today, leaving all the details to God.

I like myself, I like myself, I like myself.

I feel happy, healthy, and terrific.

I am a good person. God, you are proud of me, and you bless me with what I desire.

My Affirmation Prayers

_____

_____

_____

_____

_____

_____

_____

_____

_____

_____

_____

_____

_____

_____

_____

_____

The Fifth Great Prayer—

God, I See You Everywhere

Affirmations

God, I see you everywhere.

With the help and power of God, my life is moving in a
positive direction.

God, I see you everywhere; I can feel positive changes
happening in my life today.

God, I see your loving and positive spirit everywhere—
in my family, friends, those I work with, and
strangers.

God, I see your presence in nature—the sky, plants, and
animals—I connect to you, and I feel great!

I rejoice, I am glad, I give praise, and I give thanks.

I pray in earnest and I'm sincere; therefore I can attain
miraculous results through prayer.

Whatever things I ask for when I pray, I believe that I
already have received them, therefore I have.

When I pray, I visualize things I want and I believe I
already have them.

My Affirmation Prayers

_____

_____

_____

_____

_____

_____

_____

_____

_____

_____

_____

_____

_____

_____

_____

_____

_____

The Sixth Great Prayer—

God Bless and I Love ...

Affirmations

God bless and I love …
I pray and talk to you, God, continuously.
God bless and I love my family.
God bless and I love my friends.
God bless and I love those I am with daily.
God bless and I love all those who are in need of your
    love and strength.
I use prayer to become one with you, God, and tap into
    your power.
All day long, God, I give you praise and thanksgiving.
Thank you, God, for my daily blessings.

My Affirmation Prayers

_____

_____

_____

_____

_____

_____

_____

_____

_____

_____

_____

_____

_____

_____

_____

_____

_____

The Seventh Great Prayer—

God, Help Me Help You

Affirmations

God, help me help you.

Forgive, and I will be forgiven.

I release all negative thoughts about myself and the
world I live in.

I let go of doubt, fear, and distrust, and I quietly accept
the unknown.

God, give me purpose in my life.

God, help me do your good works here on earth today.

The more I help others and do God's work, the more
blessings I attract into my life.

My Affirmation Prayers

_____

_____

_____

_____

_____

_____

_____

_____

_____

_____

_____

_____

_____

_____

_____

_____

_____

PART SIX

Discussion Questions

Ask yourself the following questions or use them with your local 7 Great Prayers group or both. You can adapt them to use with a single prayer partner or with as large a group as you want. Remember the Seventh Great Prayer, "God, Help Me Help You." Share your experience with those around you who also seek a hopeful and blessed life.

- Before reading this book, how often did you pray? At church? At home? Before going to bed?
- Who taught you to pray?
- Before learning about affirmation prayers, how did you pray?

- Did you pray only traditional prayers?
- Did you talk with God? Do you look for signs from God for ways in which God is answering your prayers?
- Are you looking for signs from God more often now that you're doing the 21-Day Prayer Challenge?
- Are you taking walks on a regular basis?
- Are you spending quiet time with God? How are you spending this time?
- When you are in the car and at home, are you making an effort to turn off the radio? And at home, do you have the TV off, so you can spend quiet reflection time with God, using your journal?
- Are you living and thinking in a state of gratitude? How? Remember, always focus on gratitude and take your focus away from lack.
- Are you praying unceasingly? Morning, day, and night? And are you praying during the most important time, right before you go to sleep?
- Have you used The Sixth Great Prayer—"God Bless and I Love …"—on a regular basis, blessing family, friends, and coworkers? Do you bless strangers? How does this feel? Do you feel that God is always with you and with others? Does this make you feel more connected and one with God?
- Are you journaling? When? How does it make you feel?

- Are you doing the 21-Day Prayer Challenge? Have you made this commitment with a prayer partner to guarantee your success and make affirmative prayer a lifetime habit?

Additional Information

Our Web Site

Our Web site has a wealth of materials you can use in following through on your commitment to the 7 Great Prayers and the 21-Day Challenge.

Go to www.the7greatprayers.com, and you'll find:

- Journal refills
- Pocket prayer cards
- Screensaver
- More *7 Great Prayers* programs
- Materials for churches, groups, and clubs

Groups and Churches

We support book groups and prayer groups and also
have material on our Web site to facilitate the use of the
7 Great Prayers in your church or prayer group.

Share Your Story

We look forward to hearing from you. Please let us know
how *The 7 Great Prayers* helped to change your life. Your
story will be an inspiration to others. Please share at

  www.the7greatprayers.com/shareyourstory.

Newsletter

Sign up to receive weekly insight and inspiration on how
to use *The 7 Great Prayers for an Abundant and Blessed Life.*
For your free subscription, go to

  www.the7greatprayers.com/newsletter.

The 7 Great Prayers *CD*

The 7 Great Prayers CD is a great complement to the book. Play the CD in your car, on your computer or iPod, and right before you go to bed. To learn more, go to

www.the7greatprayers.com/prayercds.

About the Authors

Paul McManus has studied religion, philosophy, and self-development for more than thirty years. He has coupled his learning with inspiration from his life and family to create the 7 Great Prayers.

Paul began his career in advertising and marketing and followed the American dream of creating a better life for his wife, Tracey, and their three children. He became the president of the U.S. division of a small international software company in 1998. Life was good for the McManus family until the dot-com bubble burst. The company folded. Paul lost his job and his home. He struggled to make ends meet for his family.

Always spiritual, Paul found himself praying more and more for guidance and support during those difficult times. As material possessions slipped away, he and Tracey gave thanks and wrote *The 7 Great Prayers*. Knowing that prayer gave his family solace and strength during their challenges, Paul decided to make a career change to fulfill a higher purpose.

His mission is to teach people how to tap into the power of God and the power of the mind, to live life to its fullest through the 7 Great Prayers.

Tracey McManus is a teacher's assistant and works with elementary school children who have special needs. She also has her own photography business specializing in family portraits. The mother of three children, Tracey's passion is her family.

Married to her high school sweetheart Paul—the consummate serial entrepreneur—Tracey has experienced more than her full share of ups and downs. During the most challenging times, Tracey created a positive journal. At the end of the day, no matter how badly things might have been, she would reflect on the day and find those things that were good and give thanks for them. Recognizing the need for a tangible reminder to give thanks and pray the 7 Great Prayers, Tracey used her creative zeal and a talent for jewelry making to create *The 7 Great Prayers* blessing bracelet, blessing beads, and necklace.

By bringing people closer to God, *The 7 Great Prayers* and those jewelry beads have brought people great comfort and strength through tough times. Tracey has found purpose and joy in sharing *The 7 Great Prayers* with the world.

Paul and Tracey are using a portion of the proceeds to help homeless families and children.

The 7 Great Prayers
79 Sanford Street
Fairfield, CT 06824
www.the7greatprayers.com